Roses for New England

A Guide to Sustainable Rose Gardening

MIKE AND ANGELINA CHUTE

FORBES RIVER PUBLISHING

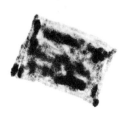

The material in this book has been carefully researched and every effort has been made to make it as accurate as possible. The authors and publisher assume no responsibility or liability to any person or entity for any errors or omissions contained in this book or for any injuries, damages, loss, or inconvenience alleged to have been caused by following the information in this book. When using any commercial product, always read and follow label directions.

Copyright © 2010 by Mike and Angelina Chute

All rights reserved. No part of this book may be reproduced or transmitted in any form or by any means, electronic or mechanical, including photocopying, recording or by any information storage and retrieval system, without written permission from the authors.

Published by Forbes River Publishing
64 Forbes Street
Riverside, RI 02915

First Edition/First Printing
Printed in the United States of America

ISBN-13: 978-0-615-33481-3

Library of Congress Control Number: 2009941288

All photographs by Mike and Angelina Chute
Cover Photo: Julia Child

To order books, visit the authors' website: www.RoseSolutions.net

Contents

Acknowledgments 4
Introduction 5

6 Know Your Roses
Chapter 1 Traits & Characteristics 9
Chapter 2 Classification 16

32 Six Basic Steps for Growing Great Roses
Chapter 3 Select Good Plants 34
Chapter 4 Start with Good Soil 41
Chapter 5 Plant in a Sunny Location 47
Chapter 6 Provide Plenty of Water 50
Chapter 7 Fertilize Frequently 55
Chapter 8 Managing Insects & Diseases 61

76 Planting, Pruning and Protecting Roses
Chapter 9 Planting 78
Chapter 10 Pruning 86
Chapter 11 Winter Protection 94

99 Sustainable Roses
Chapter 12 Sustainable Roses for New England 102

Appendix 1 Anatomy of a Rose 139
Appendix 2 Rose Societies in New England & Eastern Canada 140
Appendix 3 Public Rose Gardens in New England & Eastern Canada 141
Bibliography 142
Index 143
Book Order Form 146

Acknowledgments

We thank the following for their help and suggestions during the writing of our book: Jean M. Chute, Donna Fuss, Mike Fuss, Mike Lowe, Manuel Mendes, Jr., Peter Naumann, Emilia M. D'Andrea Nichols, Linda Shamoon, Roseanne Sherry, and Sandra Wyatt.

Introduction

Here is the book that New England gardeners have been waiting for—a detailed guide to growing roses in New England expressly written for New Englanders by New Englanders. *Roses for New England* is the first book that specifically addresses the merits and challenges of growing America's national flower in the New England area. It also emphasizes sustainability by dispelling the misconception that all roses require chemical pesticides to stay healthy.

Roses for New England is the perfect book for New England gardeners who want to grow attractive, healthy, and disease resistant roses in their home gardens. Novice rose gardeners will find everything they need to know to successfully grow roses. Experienced gardeners will utilize this book as a ready reference enabling them to grow better roses.

The idea for a rose book unique to New England began after one of our sustainable rose programs. A lady approached us and wondered why we hadn't gathered all our local horticultural know-how and written a book. That was our Eureka moment!

We knew from twenty years' experience and conducting countless rose programs that the information gardeners want the most is basic rose horticulture. We also understood that no matter what the topic of our program was, the questions at the end were always the same. What do you feed roses? How much water do they need? What do I do about Japanese beetles? What's the difference between a hybrid tea and a floribunda? How do I protect my roses in the wintertime? What's the best way to plant and prune roses?

Roses for New England not only provides complete answers to all these questions but goes much further. It explains the different types of roses and how to select the right varieties as well as inside information on how roses are propagated and marketed. It describes our six easy steps to successful rose gardening, providing details on everything that roses need to thrive. It underscores the importance of sunlight and water, what to feed roses and how often, practical choices to controlling insects and diseases, and how native New England soils can be ideal for roses with a little help. This book illustrates the proper way to plant roses, demystifies pruning, and shows how simple it is to protect them from the rigors of New England winters. It includes a comprehensive list of over 150 sustainable roses commercially available that we know will flourish in the northeast. In addition, it chronicles our rose gardening experiences through stories and personal anecdotes.

Roses for New England is a must-have book for any gardener who wants to grow beautiful roses.

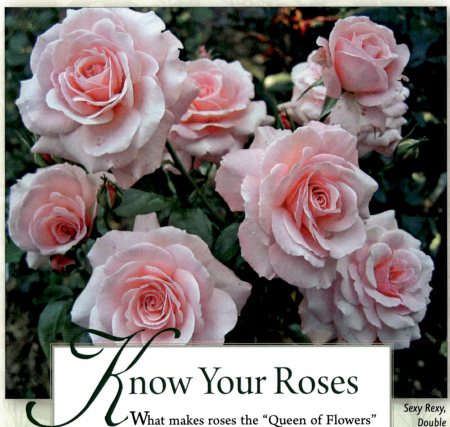

Sexy Rexy, Double

Know Your Roses

What makes roses the "Queen of Flowers" is their diversity of colors, sizes, shapes and types. In this section, we explore the different characteristics and traits that roses possess as well as how they are classified. Getting to know the various attributes of the genus *Rosa* will enable you to choose roses with confidence.

Graham Thomas, Very Double

Rhapsody in Blue, Semi-double

Sally Holmes, Single

Liebeszauber, Hybrid Tea Form

Hannah Gordon, Pink blend

Scentimental, Striped

CHAPTER 1

Traits & Characteristics

Roses come in all sizes, shapes and colors. They can have five petals or fifty, be almost any color, have button-sized rosette-shaped blooms or globe-shaped flowers as big as saucers. Roses can be once-blooming, providing a spectacular show of colors once each season or everblooming, flowering several times a season. Some roses have shiny green foliage, while some have light green matte foliage. Some are strongly fragrant and others have hardly any scent at all. Knowing about the different characteristics of roses adds to the fun of growing them and helps in planting the right roses for your garden.

Bloom Cycles

Roses may bloom once or more than once each season. *Once-blooming* roses, growing on stems and canes produced in previous seasons, have only one extended bloom period lasting several weeks. They include species roses, many old garden roses, ramblers and some large-flowered climbers. Although many other flowering plant species bloom only once a year, roses are unique in being able to bloom more than once, in fact, up to three times before it gets too cold. These repeat bloomers, mostly modern roses—hybrid teas, floribundas, miniature roses, nearly all shrub roses and large-flowered climbers—are referred to as *everblooming*. This ability to provide colorful blooms throughout the season is one of the main reasons why modern roses are so popular.

The term everblooming is somewhat misleading, implying that roses are always in bloom much the same as annuals are. The better term is *repeat blooming* or *remontant*, because repeat blooming roses produce flowers in cycles with periods of little or no bloom in-between.

The first and best bloom cycle occurs in mid-June in southern New England and seven to ten days later in the cooler north. When this bloom cycle is complete, around the Fourth of July, the spent blooms should be deadheaded to allow new stems to emerge. It takes forty to fifty days for new flowers to develop. This completes the second bloom cycle, sometime in mid-August, and when this bloom goes by, the process begins again. This will continue through autumn as long as there is adequate sunlight and the absence of an early hard frost. We get three complete bloom cycles in our shady back garden before we lose the afternoon sun behind large oak trees on neighboring property in September. A New England garden with unlimited sunlight can bloom well into the fall.

Color

Color has always been a prized characteristic and today's roses offer virtually every color in the spectrum with the exception of blue and black. Rose hybridizers endlessly cross rose varieties, dreaming of new and distinctive colors or unique variations of striped or blended colors that catch the eye and are instantly recognizable and different. Certain rose breeders have a specific color as a hybridizing objective and spend years mixing and matching varieties in the pursuit of that special hue. Tom Carruth of Weeks Roses wanted to create a true black-velvet purple and achieved it over time in stages with roses like 'Outta the Blue', 'Route 66' and 'Midnight Blue' with each newer variety becoming a darker purple than the one previous.

While plant genetics establish what color a rose will be, sunlight, plant nutrition, and weather all influence the color that we see. The warm sunrays of early morning and evening complement rose color in ways that the hard brightness of mid-day sun does not. Artists and photographers have long been aware of the affect that light has on color.

In addition to light, soil, pH, and the organic content in the soil can also affect a rose's color to the extent that the color of a rose in one garden can be subtly different from the same rose in a garden next door. Weather, especially heat, has an impact on the pigment in the petal membranes. This makes sense when you realize that only the surface of a rose petal is pigmented—a torn petal will reveal a white interior. Veteran rose gardeners know that the color of certain varieties will vary from season to season. Roses with blended color—'Double Delight' comes to mind—will demonstrate remarkable changes in color intensity between spring and fall. The light pink rose 'Pretty Lady' which has apricot-tinged inner petals in the heat of the mid-season's sun turns distinctly darker pink in the much cooler fall sun.

Robert Burns proclaimed his love was "like a red, red rose," but he most likely was indifferent towards the genetic activity responsible for the development of color. However, his famous proclamation unmistakably illustrates the complex emotional relationship between roses and romance as well as the symbolic meanings attributed to the colors of roses. Historically, white roses express purity and are used in wedding bouquets while yellow roses stand for friendship. Deep pink roses say thank you and express appreciation; light pink roses offer sympathy. Orange roses symbolize desire and passion, and everyone knows that red roses convey love and romance.

While early roses came in mostly whites, pinks, and reds, they now come in a rainbow of colors that would have amazed rosarians of a century ago. In addition to single color roses there are roses with blended colors where the petals have two or more colors that merge on the inside of each petal. The eye cannot help but be drawn to the flowers of 'Rainbow Sorbet', a blend of red and yellow, or 'Oranges 'n' Lemons', an orange and yellow blend. There are also bi-colored roses that have petals whose outside color is a different hue from that of the inside and striped roses such as 'Scentimental' with its red and white striped blooms.

With so many colors available, a gardener's choices are endless. Some may opt for a monochromatic scheme, say a bed of all white roses, which can be quite dramatic. Others may decide on a rainbow effect with a color scheme that includes every color available. When it comes to color, roses offer an enormous selection.

The American Rose Society has taken the basic colors of white, yellow, apricot, orange, pink, red, mauve and russet and divided them further into eighteen distinct color classes. They are:

White, near white, and white blend	Light pink
Light yellow	Medium pink
Medium yellow	Deep pink
Deep yellow	Pink blend
Yellow blend	Medium red
Apricot & apricot blend	Dark red
Orange & orange blend	Red blend
Orange-pink & orange pink blend	Mauve & mauve blend
Orange-red & orange red blend	Russet

Shapes

Roses come not only in diverse colors but in an assortment of shapes as well. We are all familiar with the classical hybrid tea form of a high-centered bloom that has symmetrically arranged rows of petals. This is the shape that most people associate with roses because these are the types of roses that florists sell. Other familiar rose shapes include the globular bloom that has many petals which form a ball-like circle with a closed center; a quartered shape bloom that is divided into four distinct sections; and open-cupped blooms whose petals form a cuplike flower.

Additional shapes include roses with pompom-shaped, rounded blooms comprised of many uniformly arranged short petals; and rosette-shaped blooms that are flat with many evenly arranged short petals. We enjoy a garden with roses that have various flower forms, but as with color, a rose garden with similarly shaped blooms can create a dramatic statement.

Petal Count

Petal count, another distinguishing characteristic of roses, can vary from single petaled to very double. Although one may think that the fewer the petals, the smaller the bloom, this is not necessarily the case. *Single* roses with one row of five to twelve petals, such as 'Sally Holmes', can have large blooms over three inches in diameter, while *double* roses, defined as having more than twenty-five petals in three or more rows can have small inch-and-a-half blooms as does 'Scarlet Meidiland'. *Semi-double* roses, like 'Rhapsody in Blue', have two to three rows of thirteen to twenty-five petals and 'Graham Thomas' with its *very double* blooms has more than fifty.

Petal count is often included in rose catalogue descriptions but often varies from catalogue to catalogue. However, there's no need to get caught up in the debate of whether a rose has thirty-four or thirty-eight petals or is defined as a double or semi-double. What is more relevant is that some roses have fewer petals than others. When choosing rose varieties, pay attention to petal count so that when your roses bloom, you won't be disappointed.

Foliage

Foliage can differ from variety to variety. Some varieties have glossy green or semi-glossy foliage and other varieties have matte foliage. Rose foliage may be pointed or rounded. Another variation is the color of foliage which ranges from light green to dark green to blue green.

The different colors, sizes and textures of rose foliage all add interest and diversity in a rose garden. Rugosa roses can be identified by their crinkled, textured, almost quilt-like foliage. The shiny, dark green leaves of the floribunda 'Playboy' make a powerful display against colorful red and orange-blend blooms. 'Therese Bugnet', a hybrid rugosa, and the shrub 'Rhapsody in Blue' have foliage that is a gray, blue-green which creates a pleasing palette in a garden. A number of roses, like the climber 'Clair Matin', provide color with dark reddish-purple new growth that eventually changes to green foliage with a hint of bronze green.

Fragrance

Everyone's first inclination when seeing a rose is to inhale its fragrance. Unfortunately, many of us are disappointed to find that the heady, delicious, "rose-like" fragrance of those roses reminiscent of Grandma's garden have become less characteristic of many of today's modern roses.

Although fragrance is one of the key attributes most prized by rose lovers, this quality was mainly ignored by rose breeders in the nineteenth century. Since rose hybridizing is a game of compromise, fragrance was often the victim of hybridizing objectives that concentrated on form, color, hardiness and disease resistance. In the mid-twentieth century, British hybridizer David Austin correctly predicted that if the rose-growing public were offered roses that looked and smelled like old garden roses and bloomed repeatedly all season, they would buy them in great numbers. He was right.

While fragrance is an inherited characteristic, the gene for fragrance is recessive and crossing two fragrant roses doesn't necessarily produce fragrant offspring. Despite the fickle nature of fragrance, breeders cross fragrant varieties hoping for success.

Fragrance is produced by oils in the petals of the bloom with different oils creating unique fragrances. The American Rose Society lists twenty-four distinct fragrances for roses, although the most well-known is the classic 'rose' scent. This old rose or damask scent can be found in many red and pink roses like 'Mary Rose', 'Mr. Lincoln', and 'Chrysler Imperial'. Eugenol, one of many essential oils found in roses, is responsible for a spicy, clove-like scent in the floribunda 'Ebb Tide'. Sniffing 'Graham Thomas' one may notice the light and delicate tea fragrance while "Julia Child' imparts a stronger licorice scent.

Fragrance is a subjective characteristic. Two people may smell the same rose and one may say it has a rose scent while the other identifies a tea scent. Fragrance also is influenced by temperature, humidity and the rose's stage of bloom. A fully open bloom will have more scent than a bloom that is partially open, and a rose will have a stronger scent on a warm, sunny day than on a cloudy day. Take the same rose on a cold and cloudy day, and the scent will be further reduced. Time of day also impacts a rose's fragrance. The highest concentration of oils is found in early morning which is why roses grown for their attar of roses (oils extracted from rose petals) are harvested then.

The American Rose Society awards the James Alexander Gamble Fragrance Medal to very fragrant roses. We include the list of roses that received the Gamble Fragrance Award below. This award is given to outstanding, very fragrant, new roses that are considered over a five-year period and is not necessarily awarded every year. It is interesting to note that there was an eleven-year hiatus between 1986 and 1997 when the Gamble Fragrance Award was not given. However, it was awarded in 2001, 2002, 2003, 2005, 2007 and 2008 showing that the rose industry is trying to fill the gardening public's desire for fragrant roses.

James Alexander Gamble Fragrance Medal Recipients

Rose	Type	Award Year
Crimson Glory	HT	1961
Tiffany	HT	1962
Chrysler Imperial	HT	1965
Sutter's Gold	HT	1966
Granada	HT	1968
Fragrant Cloud	HT	1970
Papa Meilland	HT	1974
Sunsprite	F	1979
Double Delight	HT	1986
Fragrant Hour	HT	1997
Angel Face	F	2001
Secret	HT	2002
Mister Lincoln	HT	2003
Sheila's Perfume	F	2005
Fragrant Plum	HT	2007
Sweet Chariot	Min	2008

CHAPTER 2

Classification

There are thousands of rose varieties with more being introduced each year and each variety is classified by type. Many of these types or classes, such as hybrid teas, shrubs, and miniature roses, may be familiar to you while other classes, like centifolias, damasks, and grandifloras, may not.

The American Rose Society designates over thirty classes of roses, but the home rose gardener does not need to have an in-depth knowledge of each and every class. Being aware of the differences between the more popular classes and their development can be helpful, though, when deciding what varieties will meet your gardening objectives. An explanation of the three main categories—species roses, old garden roses and modern roses—and some of the classes within them will shed light on the range of possibilities when considering what varieties to plant.

Species Roses

Species roses (Sp), or wild roses, are the original roses which were created from nature. All other roses developed from species roses. In botanical terms the word "species" is applied to a plant that reproduces an exact replica of itself from its own seeds. Species roses have Latin botanical names that consist of at least two parts. The first part is always *Rosa*, which refers to the genus *Rosa* to which all roses belong. The second part refers to the species itself. This name relates to either the origin of the species, as in *Rosa chinensis* which originated in China; who discovered it, for example *Rosa wichurana*, named for Max Wichura; or a specific trait it possesses, such as *Rosa multiflora* which means many-flowered. Often the word *Rosa* is abbreviated with the letter R. (*R. multiflora*) and the full Latin name is italicized.

In addition to botanical names, species roses may have common names—and sometimes more than one. Common names often vary from region to region or change over time, thus adding another factor to take into account when dealing with the identity of some species roses. *Rosa wichurana*, for example, has the common name Memorial Rose because it was often planted in cemeteries to decorate tombstones.

Most species roses require little maintenance, being very winter hardy and disease resistant. They have medium to large growth habits and are the first roses to bloom each season. As a rule, species roses have single flowers consisting of five petals (*R. sericea* is the well-known exception, having four petals), bloom once per season (although there are a few that repeat), and are known for their bright colored rose hips. *Rosa rugosa*, commonly referred to as the beach rose, can be seen along bike paths and local beaches. Another species rose often seen growing along wooded areas is *Rosa multiflora*, with its clusters of small white or pink flowers.

While no one is certain how many species roses exist, approximately 200 are said to have been recorded. Plant enthusiasts in search of roses collected samples and some kept records of their discoveries. Unfortunately, there is no assurance as to the precision of these records or that the same species was not discovered and named by different botanists. However, once commerce became common, the seeds, and sometimes the plants themselves, were transported by trading ships from one part of the world to another. New roses resulted from naturally occurring pollinization of species roses by bees or of pollen being blown from one plant to another. This was how old garden roses were first created.

Old Garden Roses

Old garden roses (OGRs) are also referred to as antique or heritage roses. The definition of OGRs is those types or classes which existed prior to 1867, the year that the first hybrid tea 'La France' was introduced. New varieties that have been hybridized after 1867 are still considered old garden roses as long as they belong to those classes that existed prior to 1867. We are fortunate that old garden roses, as a group, are extremely hardy. Many varieties, found in cemeteries and old homesteads, survived with little or no care and would have been extinct had they not possessed such hardiness and longevity.

Numerous classes fall into the group of old garden roses. The China and tea roses were unknown in Europe until trading became prominent and roses were transported in cargo ships along with tea, from the Far East to European countries. Until that time Europeans were familiar with only those classes that included damasks, albas, gallicas, centifolias, musks, and species roses. The repeat bloom of the China and tea roses made quite a sensation with Europeans who knew of only one rose, 'Autumn Damask', that bloomed twice a year. Other European roses were once-blooming. Soon rose enthusiasts were anxious to breed the Chinas and teas with European roses and the result was the creation of more classes, or types, of old garden roses.

In general, OGRs are low maintenance roses known for their fragrance, hardiness and disease resistance, although these characteristics depend on the specific variety as do their growth habit, color and flower form.

When looking at old garden roses we can divide them into the "older" OGRs versus the "newer" OGRs. The oldest of the old cultivated roses are the gallicas, damasks, and albas.

Gallica roses, once known as French roses, date back to medieval times, and the oldest rose is believed to be the species rose *R. gallica*. Gallica roses have an intense fragrance, present even when their petals are dried. They were popular for medicinal and culinary uses in Europe. The most famous gallica rose, *Rosa gallica officinalis*, also known as 'Apothecary's Rose', is noted for its use in medicine. Gallica roses are very cold hardy, disease and pest resistant and grow well even in poor soil. The bushes grow to medium height, about three feet tall, and generally have a compact habit. The foliage is dark green and the blooms range from single to many-petaled in pinks and shades of red. Most have a spicy fragrance, bloom early and only once each season.

Damask roses were enjoyed by the Greeks and Romans who were said to be avid rose gardeners. Damasks, like many OGRs, are very hardy roses characterized by intense fragrance which makes them ideal for the production of perfume. Most damasks bloom once, such as 'Celsiana', which has fragrant pink blooms that once open, quickly fade to white. An exception to the once-blooming characteristic of damask roses is 'Autumn Damask' (known in France as "Rose des Quartre Saisons"). It is a light pink, fragrant rose with a repeat bloom. One of the hardiest and most disease resistant damasks is 'Mme. Hardy', introduced in 1832. 'Mme Hardy' has large, white, fragrant, very double blooms with a striking green eye in its center. Typically, damask roses are larger than gallicas and have white or pink flowers that grow in small clusters. Their foliage is grayish-green. Damasks are able to tolerate poor soil, as well as partial shade, and are winter hardy.

Alba roses, known as "white roses" even though they come in cream and pastel shades of pink, have distinctive blue-green or grayish green foliage. They are tall, robust and elegant plants growing as high as six feet or more with very fragrant blooms that range from small to large. Albas, once-blooming plants, are able to tolerate shade and are very winter hardy, as well as disease and insect resistant. The most famous alba rose is the "White Rose of York," a pure white rose that is very fragrant. It is one of many roses grown for its essential oil, used for the production of perfume.

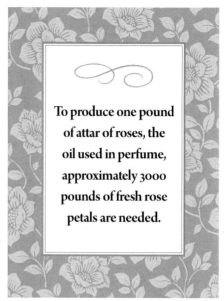

To produce one pound of attar of roses, the oil used in perfume, approximately 3000 pounds of fresh rose petals are needed.

Centifolia roses, often referred to as cabbage roses or provence roses, were hybridized by the Dutch who immortalized them in their seventeenth century paintings. Consequently, they became known as the "Rose des Peintres" (rose of the painters). Centifolias, meaning "hundred petaled," have fragrant, tightly packed, globular flowers ranging from one to four inches. The flowers grow in clusters on upright bushes with thin canes. These once-blooming roses have a sweet fragrance and are extremely winter hardy as well as disease resistant. With their semi-double to double flowers blooming in clusters on slender canes, the blooms cascade into colorful, fragrant bouquets. The downside to these blooms is that in hot, humid weather they may become soggy, unopened masses of petals.

Moss roses are easily recognized by their distinctive moss-like growth around the buds and the bases of the flowers and their strong pine-scented fragrance. It is believed that they originated as sports, or mutations, of centifolias, although later moss roses descended from the damasks. Moss roses became popular with the Victorians who depicted them in embroideries. Like centifolias, they do not tolerate heat and humidity which can cause their blooms to rot on the canes. Most varieties bloom once each season such as 'Crested Moss', also called 'Chapeau de Napoleon', a fragrant, medium pink rose. Others, such as the pink rose 'Salet', bloom in the spring and then repeats sporadically the rest of the season.

| **China** roses are descendants of the species rose *R. Chinensis* and originated in the Far East. They were introduced into Europe at the end of the eighteenth century and revolutionized the world of roses with their repeat bloom. Before the Chinas arrived in Europe the only rose known to repeat was 'Autumn Damask'. The Chinas have small blooms that grow in clusters on twiggy stems. They are not cold hardy plants and grow best in warm, dry areas such as the southeastern part of the United States as well as the Southwest. Most are too tender to grow well in New England without winter protection. 'Old Blush', also known as 'Parsons' Pink China', one of the best known of the China roses, is medium pink, disease resistant, blooms all season long and produces large orange hips when its spent blooms are not deadheaded. Descendents from China roses include the teas, Portlands, Bourbons and hybrid perpetuals.

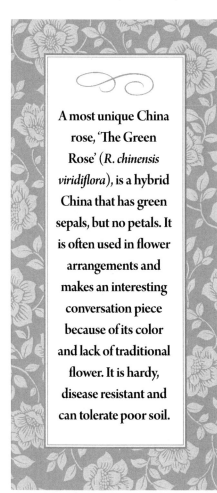

A most unique China rose, 'The Green Rose' (*R. chinensis viridiflora*), is a hybrid China that has green sepals, but no petals. It is often used in flower arrangements and makes an interesting conversation piece because of its color and lack of traditional flower. It is hardy, disease resistant and can tolerate poor soil.

| Like Chinas, **tea** roses came from the Far East, transported to Europe in cargo ships carrying tea. Chinas were the result of a cross between *R. gigantea and R. chinensis*. It is not known if they were named for their tea scent or because they were transported with tea or if they had a tea scent because they shared such close quarters with tea. (Or were they so named, one wonders, because one of their ancestors was '*R. gigentea*' which was shortened to 'tea' over time?) But, as with much to do with the history of roses, we may never know what is fact, fiction or folklore.

However, one thing is certain: tea roses became very fashionable because of their recurrent blooms. The blooms of many of the teas had high pointed centers which were distinctly different from the old fashioned, round, flat blooms found on most roses at that time. The display of these sweetly fragrant bouquets of pastel pink or yellow blooms, growing in clusters on thin, twiggy canes, endeared the tea roses to the Victorians despite the fact that they were very tender. Many tea roses had to be grown in conservatories because of their lack of cold hardiness which makes them unsuitable to grow in New England.

Portland roses are a small class of roses descended from gallica, damask and China roses, although their origin is a matter of debate among rosarians. The first Portland rose, the 'Duchess of Portland', appeared in France sometime prior to 1800. It is thought to be a cross between the very fragrant 'Autumn Damask' and 'Apothecary's Rose' and possibly an unknown China. Regardless of its parentage, the result is a fragrant, large, many-petaled flower with an almost continual bloom throughout the season. Portland roses are small, compact bushes with an upright habit. They have grayish-green foliage, like the damasks, and produce fragrant blooms that repeat all season. 'Rose de Rescht', classified as a Portland rose by the American Rose Society, grows very well in southern New England. When cut and brought inside, the fragrant, magenta colored blooms fill a room with their scent.

Bourbon roses resulted from a natural cross between the China rose 'Old Blush' and the damask rose 'Quartre Saison', that were growing in close proximity to each other on the Ile de Bourbon (now called Reunion) located in the Indian Ocean. Bourbon roses appeared in France in the early 1800's and were the first variety developed from the hybrid Chinas that had repeat bloom. Because of their repeat bloom they were of great interest to hybridizers who used them to create new, repeat-blooming varieties. Some Bourbon roses mimic their damask ancestry with a compact, shrub-like habit while others take after the China bloodline growing long, flexible canes. They produce fragrant, cupped or quartered blooms but, as a class, are susceptible to the fungal disease blackspot. An exception to this is 'Souvenir de la Malmaison', (named after the home of Napoleon's wife Josephine), which is moderately disease resistant. In contrast to the blush pink, fragrant, shrub-like 'Souvenir de la Malmaison', which grows no more than four feet high, 'Zephirine Drouhin', a thornless, fragrant pink rose, has a climbing habit and can grow up to twelve feet tall. Although happiest in warmer climates, Bourbon roses are cold hardy in this area with winter protection.

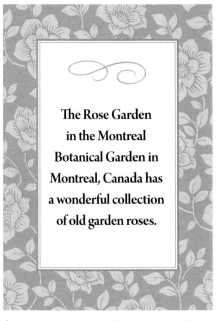

The Rose Garden in the Montreal Botanical Garden in Montreal, Canada has a wonderful collection of old garden roses.

Noisette roses had their origin in the United States in 1811. The first Noisette was hybridized by John Champneys from Charlestown, South Carolina who crossed 'Old Blush' with the musk rose *R. moschata*. The result was a light pink, fragrant rose named 'Champneys' Pink Cluster'. Champneys gave these seedlings to his neighbor, Philippe Noisette who, after making some crosses of his own, sent the seedlings to his brother, Louis, who lived in Paris. Louis named the first seedling after his brother and, voila, the Noisette roses were born.

Noisette roses have both a climbing and shrub-like habit. The flowers are very fragrant, grow in small clusters, and are mostly white, pink or yellow. They are tender plants, doing best in warm weather climates and are prone to blackspot. Since they are not winter hardy, avoid planting Noisettes in New England.

Hybrid perpetual roses were produced by crossing existing hybrid classes, notably the Bourbons, hybrid Chinas, Noisettes and Portlands. They are tall, upright plants with large, full blooms that show the characteristics of their ancestor—notably Bourbon roses. They produce a heavy first bloom with a lighter second bloom which is followed by another heavy fall bloom. The colors of hybrid perpetuals are mainly white, pink and crimson. 'Baronne Prevost', a very fragrant hybrid perpetual, has medium pink, double blooms and is winter hardy to Zone 5. Unfortunately, it is prone to blackspot. Another popular hybrid perpetual is 'Paul Neyron', a vigorous rose which produces large blooms on strong upright canes on bushes that can grow as tall as seven feet.

Although hybrid perpetuals caught the fancy of gardeners in the United States and were widely grown, they lost their popularity with the introduction of hybrid tea roses in 1867 when the era of modern roses began.

Modern Roses

The history of modern roses began in 1867 with the introduction of what is considered the first hybrid tea rose, 'La France'. This new class was the result of a cross between a hybrid perpetual and a tea rose.

Hybrid tea roses, hardier than the teas and producing more repeat blooming than the hybrid perpetuals, dramatically changed the world of roses with their high-centered, formal blooms. They provided a wide range of colors not found in the familiar old garden roses and, most importantly, hybrid teas presented rose lovers with the much sought-after repeat bloom cycle.

Hybrid tea roses quickly became the rose of choice in gardens during the late nineteenth century and they still remain popular today. Hybrid teas grow straight and tall, producing one bloom at the end of each long stem. This, plus the classic form of their blooms—several rows of petals spiraling up and around a raised center—makes them distinctive and perfect to display in vases and arrangements. Their ability to rebloom every forty to sixty days in a wide range of colors made them the dominant class of roses for over 140 years.

While some hybrid teas are very fragrant, like the dark red 'Mister Lincoln' and the more contemporary red blend 'Double Delight', most have little or no fragrance, a compromise made by hybridizers seeking color and flower form. This came at a price, though, with disease resistance being sacrificed along with fragrance. Hybrid teas, by and large, require a high level of maintenance and since they are prone to fungal diseases often rely on a chemical spray program to keep them healthy and looking their best. Many varieties are not hardy enough to survive even a mild New England winter on their own, making winter protection mandatory.

At one time we grew many more hybrid teas than we do now, but gradually we

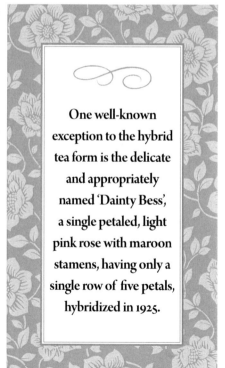

One well-known exception to the hybrid tea form is the delicate and appropriately named 'Dainty Bess', a single petaled, light pink rose with maroon stamens, having only a single row of five petals, hybridized in 1925.

replaced most of them with more sustainable varieties. We still include a few in our gardens because their elegant blooms and saturated color are worth a little extra work. The pink and very fragrant 'The McCartney Rose' is a long-time favorite as is 'Tineke', with its creamy white, ruffled blooms. 'Dublin', a medium red with perfect hybrid tea form and unique smoky edges to the petals, still remains in our garden along with 'Marijke Koopman', a pink beauty that repeats quickly on very long stems. We add a little extra winter protection in the fall and provide a program to control fungal diseases to these hybrid teas.

Polyanthas, the predecessors of floribundas, are extremely hardy and disease resistant roses that bloom throughout the season. Although their origin is often the source of debate among rosarians, we know that in the late nineteenth century polyanthas were developed in France from crossing *Rosa multiflora* with a dwarf China rose. The results were very floriferous plants that had small, cabbage-like roses growing in clusters on short stems. Most polyanthas have white or pink blooms. The polyantha 'Mlle. Cecile Brunner', also called the Sweetheart Rose, dates back to 1881 and has moderately fragrant, small, light pink flowers that grow in large clusters. 'The Fairy', introduced in 1932, is another light pink polyantha often seen in New England gardens where it produces hundreds of small blooms all season, needing very little care when it comes to insects and diseases.

Floribundas, originally called hybrid polyanthas, are a result of crossing hybrid teas with polyanthas and date back to the 1920's when the Poulsens from Denmark introduced 'Rodhatte' (Red Riding Hood). The term floribunda was used by Jackson & Perkins but was not adapted by the American Rose Society until 1952. Eugene Boerner, a hybridizer who worked at Jackson & Perkins, developed so many floribundas that he is known in rose circles as "Papa Floribunda."

Floribundas, meaning "many flowered," are sturdy, floriferous plants. They have abundant blooms growing in sprays, or clusters, a trait inherited from the polyanthas, but on longer stems, a trait of hybrid teas. While some varieties have blooms with hybrid tea form, others have cupped or flat blooms that are reminiscent of the blooms of old garden roses. Floribundas are smaller, shorter and more compact than hybrid teas, often with shrubby, spreading habits but with larger blooms and a larger growth habit than polyanthas. While they are ideal as all-purpose landscape plants, many varieties with their dazzling, colorful blooms and hybrid tea form look impressive planted alone or in small groups of three or five. Not only are floribundas recurrent, some varieties recycle so quickly they seem to have color all season. Floribundas tend to be hardier and more disease resistant than hybrid teas.

One of our favorite floribundas that does extremely well in our shady garden is 'Blueberry Hill'. It is a compact bush with shiny, dark green foliage that creates a stunning backdrop for its lavender blooms with yellow stamens. 'Julia Child', introduced in 2004, a disease resistant floribunda with a licorice fragrance, has clusters of pure yellow blooms that look magnificent on the bush as well as in a vase. 'Super Hero' is an extremely sustainable floribunda that was introduced in 2008. Its dark red flowers with 35 to 40 petals mimic hybrid tea form until they fully open into lush, satiny blooms. Since floribundas have many varieties that are disease resistant and winter hardy, producing flowers that bloom almost continuously, they are an excellent option for gardeners looking for roses that are sustainable and easy to grow.

Grandiflora is a class of modern roses that is very similar to the hybrid tea which is not surprising since grandifloras are the result of crossing hybrid teas with floribundas. Most grandifloras are tall, recurrent bushes. Their blooms have the high-centered form of hybrid teas, and while grandifloras can grow one bloom on long, straight stems, they also produce sprays like floribundas.

The first and best known grandiflora is 'Queen Elizabeth', introduced in 1954. It is a tall plant with dark green, glossy foliage and large pink blooms growing in clusters. Other popular grandifloras include 'Cherry Parfait' that has stunning white petals with bright red edges and 'Crimson Bouquet' which produces large, dark red sprays of flowers amid immaculate, dark green foliage.

Shrub roses form a very broad class and typically demonstrate above-average hardiness and disease resistance, making them ideal choices for any rose garden. While they have an informal, relaxed growth habit that is larger than that of hybrid teas and floribundas, they include small landscape varieties, too. Shrubs come in a wide range of colors and sizes and most repeat several times per season. The flowers range from simple five-petaled singles like 'Home Run' and 'Sally Holmes' to flowers with 60 or more petals, like the very double pink flowers of 'Heritage'. The bloom shape is typically open, exposing the stamens as opposed to the high centers found in hybrid teas.

New England gardeners have a wide selection of shrubs to choose from like the popular David Austin English roses known for their fragrant, old-fashioned flowers and repeat bloom. We have a specimen planting of Austin's 'Graham Thomas' that has grown in our garden for many years. Its June bloom is a stunning display of buttery yellow blooms—four to six to a spray—with another lighter bloom to look forward to later in the season.

The tough Canadian Explorer series of shrub roses are extremely winter hardy and grow three to four feet high in frigid Canada. In southern New England's moderate Zone 6 they explode to double that size. If you have enough room you may want to consider the Explorer rose 'William Baffin', a deep pink shrub that has excellent disease resistance and can be grown as either a climber or a bush. Other hardy and disease resistant shrubs include Buck roses, developed at Iowa State University by Griffith Buck. Buck's 'Carefree Beauty' with its semi-double pink blooms grows well without the use of any pesticides. 'Bonica', introduced in 1987 by Meilland International, and the first shrub to receive the All America Rose Selection (AARS) award, is another pink, very hardy, disease resistant shrub rose. Many other Meilland roses are also sustainable

The popular red 'Knock Out' (hybridized by William Radler) and other members of the 'Knock Out' family are very disease resistant. 'Double Knock Out', which has blooms with twice as many petals and longer stems than 'Knock Out', and the pink 'Blushing Knock Out' are "bullet proof" shrubs, too. We especially like 'Sunny Knock Out' with its yellow, single flowers that have a light fragrance.

The Easy Elegance collection hybridized by Ping Lim from Bailey Nurseries in Minnesota offers other disease resistance shrubs. 'My Hero' has massive displays of bright red blooms, good disease resistance and is hardy to Zone 4. Growing in our sustainable garden with excellent results and no

> The American Rose Society divides shrub roses into two types, classic and modern. Classic shrubs include the classes hybrid rugosa, hybrid kordesii, hybrid moyesii, and hybrid musk because varieties in these classes have a species rose in their near background. All other shrub roses are considered modern shrub roses. For our purposes, however, we refer to all the ARS sub-classes under the broad class of shrubs.

chemical pesticides are the Easy Elegance shrubs 'All the Rage' with apricot flowers and yellow centers and 'My Girl' with deep pink, ruffled blooms.

Shrubs having rugose (wrinkled) foliage belong to a class called **hybrid rugosa**, a result of crossing wild rugosa roses with other types of roses. These shrubs are a perfect choice for the New England gardener looking for sustainable roses. As a class, they tolerate not only bitter cold, but salt water and poor soil. They are highly disease resistant and require no pesticides. In fact, spraying damages their foliage. We planted hybrid rugosas as a hedge along a chain link fence and their vigorous growth hid most of the fence in just two seasons. 'Hansa', a thorny, sprawling bush that grows seven feet high and six feet wide, rewards us with fragrant, large, red blooms, and during the winter we enjoy its large, colorful rose hips. 'Therese Bugnet', another hybrid rugosa, has a more upright habit than 'Hansa' and grows just as tall. It has ruffled pink, fragrant flowers and a copious early bloom, followed by a lighter repeat. An added benefit is the interest it gives to the winter landscape with canes and foliage that turn red in the fall.

The complaint against shrub roses has been a lack of fragrance and non-descript blooms growing on short stems. However, rose breeders began to recognize the long-term commercial value of shrubs and the rose-buying public's demand for easy care, sustainable, fragrant roses. This has led to a dramatic improvement in the development of shrub roses with longer stems, more fragrance, and more complex flowers, without losing their above average disease resistance.

Miniature roses are propagated as rooted cuttings and grow on their own roots giving them a winter hardy toughness that belies their size. They grow from six inches to over thirty-six inches tall. Smaller versions of larger roses, they come in a wide range of color, from white to deep, dark red, with many possessing hybrid tea-like form. What makes "minis" interesting is that they have miniature blooms and proportionately miniature foliage regardless of the size of the plant.

While miniature or "dwarf" roses were popular in the 1800's, they almost disappeared from commerce as other types of roses, such as the hybrid perpetuals, replaced them in popularity. However, as rose lore has it, in 1918 a dwarf rose was discovered in Geneva by a soldier named Roulet. The rose was named 'Rouletii', after the soldier, and later crossed with a polyantha rose by the Dutch hybridizer deVink. The result was a red miniature rose with a white eye called 'Peon' whose name was changed to 'Tom Thumb' when introduced in the United States in 1936. 'Tom Thumb' was used in the breeding of many subsequent miniature roses. Californian hybridizer Ralph Moore is responsible for introducing numerous miniature roses and is credited as the "father of miniature roses." Today hundreds of varieties of miniature roses are in commerce.

Miniature roses are perfect for the small garden or containers, including window boxes as well as hanging planters. 'Jeanne Lajoie', a pink climbing miniature, produces clusters of hundreds of tiny many-petaled flowers. Its habit, with cascading stems, makes it ideal to plant in a container. 'Behold', another miniature perfect for growing in a container, has clear yellow hybrid tea-like blooms creating an impressive contrast against its lush green foliage.

In the 1970's, miniature roses were introduced that had blooms and foliage larger than those on typical miniatures, but smaller than those found on floribundas. J. Benjamin Williams trademarked the term Mini-Flora and donated its use to the American Rose Society who adopted the class Mini-Flora in 1999. There are now numerous Mini-Flora roses being introduced each year.

Climbing roses have the genetic disposition to grow canes long enough to train up an arbor or trellis or along a fence and add a vertical dimension to any garden. Since they are not true "climbers," having no tendrils that can cling and wrap themselves around a support, their canes need to be tied to a supporting structure. There are two groups of climbing roses: large-flowered climbers and hybrid wichuranas, formerly classified as ramblers.

During the 1950's, Walter Brownell and his wife Josephine developed a series of Everblooming Pillars in Little Compton, RI. Their Everblooming Pillars are large-flowered climbers that repeat regularly on the current year's growth. Most varieties were identified by a number until they were introduced and then given a name. For example, Everblooming Pillar No. 3 went on to become 'White Cap'. These vintage roses hybridized in Rhode Island over a half century ago continue to demonstrate excellent winter hardiness as well as above average disease resistance.

Hybrid wichuranas have long, thin, supple canes that produce large clusters of small, once-blooming flowers. 'Dorothy Perkins' introduced in 1901 is the most well-known **rambler** and displays small pink flowers that grow in large clusters.

Large-flowered climbers have long, stiff canes and large flowers, as the name suggests, that grow on lateral canes. Most are everblooming such as 'New Dawn', a fragrant, pale pink climber with canes capable of growing 10 to 12 feet tall and just as wide. Its flowers of 35 to 40 petals create a lovely contrast against glossy, dark green foliage. The first rose to bloom in our Rhode Island garden is the large-flowered climber 'Clair Matin'. It grows well over eight feet tall, producing soft pink blooms with golden yellow stamens and creates the focal point in our garden with its mass of color by mid-June.

Tree roses, or standards, are not a separate class but any variety that is grafted onto a tall stem or trunk. Traditionally, tree roses are not winter hardy because the bud union, the most vulnerable part of a rose, is exposed well above the soil line, making them difficult to protect during New England winters. However, the introduction of own-root tree roses will eliminate this problem. 'Polar Joy', an own-root tree rose developed specifically for northern gardens by Ping Lim, was introduced in 2006 and is not only disease resistant, but hardy to Zone 4. With the introduction of own-root tree roses, New England gardeners will be able to incorporate vertical height to even small gardens that can not accommodate larger climbing roses.

Sports

A *sport* is a naturally occurring genetic mutation, a part of a plant that is different from the rest of the plant. It comes from the Middle English word *desporten* which in turn comes from the Old French *desporter* meaning "to divert."

The most common sports of roses are changes in growth habit—from bush type to climbers—and changes in color. The white floribunda 'Iceberg' and the famous hybrid tea 'Peace' are two of many bush type varieties that sported climbing forms (appropriately named 'Climbing Iceberg' and 'Climbing Peace') that were introduced as new varieties.

Color sports are more common than you would think. Some are very subtle and go unnoticed, often attributed to environmental factors or change of season. Others are hard to miss. A glittering pink sport of the pure white 'Iceberg' was discovered in Tasmania and introduced as 'Brilliant Pink Iceberg' in 2001. 'Brilliant Pink Iceberg', in turn, created its own deep purple and cream sport which was introduced as 'Burgundy Iceberg'. All have the same bushy habit, great sprays, glossy green foliage and nearly thornless stems.

Alterations in remondancy (repeat bloom) and petal count occur, too, but are far less common. Arguably, the most famous rose sport was the discovery by Henry Dreer in 1930 of a repeating stem growing on a bush of a once-blooming climber named 'Dr. W. Van Fleet'. The repeat-blooming stem was removed from the bush then rooted and, after a trial period to test its stability, was introduced as 'New Dawn'. It maintained the same soft pink, lightly fragrant blooms, rowdy growth habit and cast iron constitution as 'Dr. W. Van Fleet' but became more desirable because of its repeat bloom. 'New Dawn', with 30 to 40 petals, sported still another variation with twice as many petals and was introduced as 'Awakening'.

Generally, a sport is not as good a plant as its parent. Sports are notoriously unstable, frequently reverting back to its original form. For that reason, commercial growers are suspicious of sports and extensively field test the very few sports they even consider for introduction. While the vast majority of sports remain anonymous curiosities, a very few do get introduced occasionally. Both 'Pink Knockout' and 'Blushing Knockout', color sports of their well-known cousin' Knockout', eventually joined this famous family of roses.

Abbreviation Key of the Genus Rosa

Species Roses — Sp

Old Garden Roses — OGR

Alba	A
Bourbon	B
Centifolia	C
Damask	D
Hybrid China	HCh
Gallica	G
Hybrid Perpetual	HP
Hybrid Spinosissima	HSpn
Moss	M
Noisette	N
Portland	P
Tea	T

Modern Roses

Floribunda	F
Grandiflora	Gr
Hybrid Kordesii	HKor (Classic Shrub)
Hybrid Moyesii	HMoy (Classic Shrub)
Hybrid Musk	HMsk (Classic Shrub)
Hybrid Rugosa	HRg (Classic Shrub)
Hybrid Tea	HT
Hybrid Wichurana	HWich (formerly Rambler)
Large-Flowered Climber	LCl
Miniature	Min
Mini-Flora	MinFl
Polyantha	Pol
Shrub	S (Modern Shrubs)

Weeks Rose Fields

Six Basic Steps for Growing Great Roses

Growing roses can be fun. Just follow our six easy steps that provide roses with everything they need. Our steps are simple: select good plants; develop rich, organic soil; plant in a sunny location; supply plenty of water; establish a monthly fertilizing schedule; and employ a pest management program. This section explains each step and illustrates in detail everything you need to know to grow roses better than you ever thought you could.

Raised bed

Pretty Lady

All the Rage

Rhode Island Red and White Cap

CHAPTER 3

STEP 1:
Select Good Plants

Millions of roses are sold in the United States every year. Thousands of varieties of hybrid teas, grandifloras, floribundas, climbers, shrubs, and old garden roses are grown row-after-row in great fields in California, Arizona, and Texas. They are harvested in late fall, then graded and packed by variety in bundles of five or ten, and later stored in mammoth climate-controlled facilities for shipment to retailers across the nation the following winter and spring. With such an enormity of choice, how do you select the right varieties for your garden?

While each of us has personal criteria for choosing rose varieties for our gardens, the first consideration for a New England garden should be the selection of winter hardy roses. Simply put, winter hardiness is the ability of a plant to remain dormant and successfully survive cold weather. Roses that are unable to adapt to typical New England winters, even with some winter protection, are too tender and should not be chosen regardless of their other desirable traits.

Based on the USDA Plant Hardiness Zone Map, roses and other plants are sorted by the coldest temperatures that they can endure without injury. This map divides North America into eleven zones based on the average annual minimum temperature in each zone, using data collected over a sixty-year span. Zone 1, which includes Fairbanks, Alaska with an average minimum temperature of -50°F, is the coldest. Zone 11, which includes Honolulu, Hawaii with an average minimum temperature of over 40°F, is the warmest.

Northernmost areas of Maine, Vermont, and New Hampshire are Zones 3b and 4a. *(See New England Plant Hardiness Zone Map.)* We have been in the mountains of western Maine in January many times and can attest that it is one of the coldest places in New England. Rose gardeners there plant very hardy shrub roses, old garden roses, and species roses. They consider hybrid teas as annuals. Central New England, from mid-Maine, middle sections of New Hampshire and Vermont down through western Massachusetts are mainly Zones 4b and 5a. Species roses, most shrub and old garden roses, and miniature roses will thrive here. Hybrid teas, floribundas, grandifloras, and many climbers will grow here too, but are less hardy and require winter protection to survive. Connecticut is primarily Zone 6a but has colder areas of Zone 5b in pockets up in the northeast and northwest corners. The plant hardiness map places Rhode Island

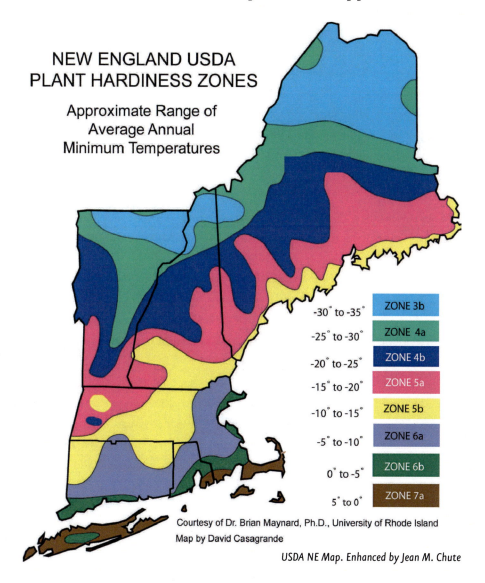

Courtesy of Dr. Brian Maynard, Ph.D., University of Rhode Island
Map by David Casagrande

USDA NE Map. Enhanced by Jean M. Chute

squarely in Zone 6a and 6b. But some areas in the northern tip are recognized as Zone 5b and a sliver of southern coastline is defined as Zone 7a, giving the smallest state in the Union an amazing four-zone spread. While almost any rose can be grown in southern New England, it's a good idea to provide some degree of winter protection to hybrid teas, grandifloras, and floribundas. Nevertheless, some classes of roses, such as most varieties of teas, Chinas, and Noisettes, will not survive typical New England winters at all.

While the zone map is a good general hardiness indicator, it is not perfect. It does not factor in the effects of rainfall, sunlight, wind, and humidity. It cannot measure the benefit of snow cover or the damage inflicted by freeze and thaw cycles and it does not account for different microclimates within a zone.

Other local indicators can determine a rose's ability to survive New England winters. A visit to public rose gardens will show which varieties are robust and thriving and which are struggling. Local rose societies are superb sources of rose horticulture and can provide very specific recommendations regarding the best winter hardy varieties for their areas. *(See Appendix for a list of rose societies and public gardens.)*

After winter hardiness, the second factor to consider is whether you want to have a sustainable rose garden or a garden that will require chemical pesticides. Our criteria for sustainability is two-fold: the variety must be winter hardy (see above) and it must have a demonstrated resistance to common rose diseases, particularly fungal diseases. Sustainable roses, then, are those varieties that will remain healthy and attractive in your garden without the use of chemical pesticides. On the other hand, if you decide to have a garden planted with hybrid teas or other varieties that are not disease resistant, then this lack of sustainability will require you to employ chemical pesticides. If you want sustainable, easy care roses, consider the wide selection of disease resistant modern shrubs, floribundas, and old garden roses that can be just as satisfying with less work. *(See Chapter 12 for our list of sustainable roses.)*

We have both kinds of rose gardens. In our older, established garden we initially planted hybrid teas, non-sustainable floribundas and other varieties that we sprayed on a regular basis. Although we stopped using insecticides several years ago, we currently continue to use fungicides to control fungal diseases. However, we are steadily decreasing the number of times we spray each season due to our gradual shift away from varieties that are susceptible to diseases. We are replacing these varieties with tougher, disease resistant modern shrub roses and floribundas. When we planned the second rose garden, we chose to plant only sustainable varieties and include perennials, annuals, herbs, and other plant species.

Knowing which varieties are resistant to garden pests is the key in selecting roses for a sustainable garden, but it is also important to realize that a rose that is disease resistant in one garden may be less so in another garden. Such was the case with 'Zephirine Drouhin', a pink, fragrant Bourbon, known to have above average disease resistance. It developed a bad case of powdery mildew when we planted it as a climber in a new sustainable rose garden we recently designed. We replaced it with the reliable 'New Dawn' that performed much better. 'Abbaye de Cluny', a lovely apricot hybrid tea that grew fungus-free without pesticides in a municipal garden in Providence, RI, became badly infected with blackspot and completely defoliated when we planted it in another public garden nearby. Part of this can be explained by realizing that fungal diseases come in more than one strain. Blackspot, for instance, has a number of strains and a sustainable rose may be resistant to a strain found in one garden but less resistant to a different strain found in another. Ultimately, the degree of resistance of any variety will be determined in large measure by the prevailing conditions in your garden.

Third, decide where your roses will be planted and how much room they will need. Choose plants whose size (height and width) and growth habit (shape) will fill the allotted space nicely when they are fully grown. A common error is underestimating the mature size of rose varieties and having to move large plants that have quickly outgrown their spots in the garden. We have one friend who tells the story of planting what she thought was a cute little rose along the patio behind her home and two years later hacking it down before it ate her neighbor's fence.

Growth habit and size are often included in catalog descriptions, but sizes given are only approximations and will vary widely from region to region throughout the country. For example, 'William Baffin', a rough, tough shrub rose that grows three to four feet tall in Canada where it was hybridized, explodes to eight feet tall and just as wide in Rhode Island's moderate Zone 6. Not all garden centers have experienced rosarians on staff but some do, and it won't hurt to ask about size and growth habit when making rose selections.

While keeping sustainability, hardiness, disease resistance, size, and growth habit in mind, choose the type of rose that is "right" for your garden. What other qualities have the greatest appeal to you? Do you want roses with stems long enough to cut and enjoy indoors? What about landscape roses for mass plantings? Is fragrance important? Do you want roses with repeat blooms? What colors do you like? What kind of blooms do you prefer, modern or old fashioned? What are your expectations and how much effort will you provide to achieve it?

While mulling over these factors, identify the best local nurseries, garden centers and good online mail-order sources for roses. Join a local rose society and attend monthly meetings to sound out veteran rose gardeners who are more than willing to give you the local lowdown on roses.

After the New Year, rose catalogs begin to arrive full of glossy photographs and lavish descriptions of each variety with an emphasis on the always-incredible new introductions. While these descriptions are often superb examples of creative writing, they also contain useful facts that can be gleaned from careful reading. They identify color, often in great detail; plant size or growth habit; bloom size including petal count; fragrance, if any; and some may even include the hybridizer and parentage as well as the degree of winter hardiness and disease resistance. However, claims of disease resistance, especially in rose catalogs, may be exaggerated and will often describe a rose as being resistant to disease which may or may not be the case. If a catalog says nothing at all about a variety's disease resistance, do not assume that it is; research that rose further.

Rose catalogs are good resources and effective marketing tools. We enjoy discovering the interesting names that roses are given as well as all the other information included in the descriptions. In fact, we occasionally buy a variety solely because we like its name. We have had mixed results with this very unscientific approach to rose selection, but it is fun to do once in a while. Years ago we discovered a shrub rose called 'Angelina' and bought it because of the name. The rose grew so badly that first season that we shovel-pruned it directly into the trash barrel. We would not even give it away. On the other hand, though, we have had good luck with names, too. Based on their names we bought, planted, and still grow, 'Playboy', 'Passionate Kisses', 'The McCartney Rose', and recently 'Julia Child', and they are all terrific roses.

After you have made a list of roses to purchase, decide whether to buy them locally or through mail order sources. We buy both ways with good results.

When ordering from catalogs, expect to receive *bareroot roses*—dormant roses without soil on their roots. Mail order roses are almost always shipped as bare root plants packed in some lightweight, moisture-holding, non-soil material or wrapped in plastic bags. What we like about mail-order roses is the additional choices they provide beyond local nurseries, especially with hard-to-find varieties. For this reason, we frequently order roses for both spring and fall delivery from a few favorite online mail order sources. These varieties are shipped at the correct time and arrive in perfect condition just in time for planting which should be soon after delivery.

New England nurseries and garden centers sell *container-grown* roses that are bare-root roses potted up prior to sale. Container-grown roses give you the opportunity to observe roses as growing plants after they have left dormancy. You are able to evaluate the new stems, foliage, buds, and even blooms as well as the rose's overall general health. A container-grown rose offers you the option of planting at your convenience. If necessary, roses can be left in containers for an entire season, but they should be repotted in a size larger container to prevent them from becoming root bound. We often grow roses in containers for one season, occasionally for two, to test new varieties and see if they deserve a spot in our garden. Eventually, all roses should be planted in the ground where they always grow best.

When buying from local nurseries and garden centers, consider those that have a reputation for selling quality plants. These plant merchants often have experienced horticulturists available to answer questions and guide you towards the best choices for your garden. Regardless of where you shop for container-grown roses, choose healthy plants. Look for fresh, green, unwrinkled canes and, although roses do get nicked somewhat during harvesting and handling, steer clear of bushes with spots, lesions, blemishes or other signs of disease. As you decide which plants to take home, learn to recognize and understand the various methods used to produce and grade roses.

The two primary methods of commercial asexual rose propagation, the multiplying of new plants of the same variety, are grafting and rooting.

When a bud eye from the variety to be reproduced is joined, or grafted, onto the main cane, or shank, of another rose bush, called an understock or rootstock, the result is a *grafted rose*. The site of this grafting becomes swollen and is referred to as the *bud union*. Rootstock, which increases the vigor and hardiness of a variety, provides a root system that is already fully developed. Grafted roses are field grown for two seasons before harvesting and most hybrid teas, grandifloras, and floribundas are propagated this way.

After harvesting, grafted roses are graded on a set of standards based on size and quality established by the American Association of Nurserymen. Look for the grade on the label, in the catalog, or ask at the garden center or when placing an order.

- Number 1 is the highest grade in the industry. It has three or more canes growing from the bud union, each having a diameter at least as thick as a pencil—thicker is better. The length of the canes should be fifteen to eighteen inches although length is not critical. The canes are pruned by the grower at the time of harvest and may be re-pruned again by the retailer to stimulate growth.

- Number 1½ is the same as number 1, but with only two canes, and represents good value when sold at a discount.
- Number 2 is a cull and not recommended.

Creating *own-root roses* is a simple method of rose propagation which is done by inserting sections of young rose stems, called softwood cuttings, into a growing medium where they will take root. Roses grown on their own roots are often extra hardy and quicker and less expensive to produce. While own-root roses may start off smaller than grafted roses, they will quickly catch up. Miniature roses and many shrub and old garden roses are reproduced this way.

Which method is better? It depends on the type and variety. Hybrid teas and grandifloras almost always perform much better as grafted plants while miniature roses will thrive as rooted cuttings. We have seen many varieties of floribundas successfully propagated both ways. The great Canadian Explorer shrub roses start as rooted cuttings and growing on their own roots adds to their already considerable hardiness. Through years of testing, commercial rose growers have developed the most efficient methods to produce the strongest plants and you will find excellent roses propagated both ways available in local garden centers and through mail-order sources. In the end, if a rose bush is fresh, healthy, and growing true to form, then it makes no difference how it was propagated.

Rose Buyers Check List

1. **Choose varieties that are sustainable—winter hardy and disease resistant.**
2. **Buy the "right" rose with the best growth habit for the space you have.**
3. **Check local public rose gardens and catalogs for varieties you like.**

CHAPTER 4

STEP 2:
Start with Good Soil

Every gardener agrees that successful rose cultivation starts with good soil. Soil serves as the medium that anchors a plant's roots and through which water, nutrients and oxygen are supplied. Although roses are versatile and resilient plants, able to grow in a wide variety of soils, they will grow best if given a porous, well-balanced soil rich with organics.

It's not necessary to be an expert on soil to grow good roses, but it helps to have a basic understanding of the composition of soil. Simply put, the makeup of soil consists of a mixture of mineral particles derived from eroded rock—sand, clay, and silt—plus organic matter. *Sand* is the largest particle found in soil. Between each sand particle are relatively large spaces allowing water to pass through the soil quickly, which provides excellent drainage and aeration. But the downside of sandy soil is that as water drains, it carries water soluble nutrients away. The smallest particle is *clay*. These particles cling tightly together, holding in water and nutrients. The problem with clay soil is that water drains through it slowly and it has poor aeration. The size of *silt* particles fall between that of sand and clay. Silt provides good drainage and, at the same time, it retains many nutrients. The organic matter component of soil makes it more porous, improving its water holding capacity while enabling it to drain well.

Some areas in New England have soil that already possesses many of the necessary properties of good garden soil. For example, Rhode Island soil generally exhibits a light, sandy texture from sand and silt. Other areas along the Connecticut River Valley contain clay. Amend either type of soil with enough organic matter and it becomes perfect for cultivating roses.

If we were to wish for the best medium for roses it would be a rich, organic topsoil sometimes referred to as "loam" (pronounced as "loom" by native New Englanders). The ideal topsoil would consist of a mixture of sand and clay plus abundant amounts of organic matter that holds water without getting soggy and won't dry out too quickly. This combination provides spaces within the soil for both air and water to penetrate. Since the composition of soil can vary significantly even in the same general location, have your soil tested. A soil test determines the condition of soil, including pH, soil texture, organic matter content, macro and micronutrients, and even offers corrective measures. Some state universities, such as the University of Massachusetts, offer soil tests. *(See Testing pH below.)*

pH

pH, the measure of acidity/alkalinity in the soil, has a direct effect on the ability of plants to absorb nutrients, yet many gardeners are unaware of its importance. pH can be determined with either a simple pH test or as part of a complete soil test. It is expressed on a scale of 1 to 14 with 7 being neutral. Readings below 7 are considered acidic and those above 7 are alkaline. Note well that each number on the scale represents a tenfold difference from the next. For instance, a pH of 5 is ten times more acidic than a pH of 6 and a hundred times more acidic than a pH of 7. If the soil is too acidic, nutrients become insoluble and cannot be absorbed. Also, beneficial microorganisms in the soil, which break down organic matter making nutrients available, are less able to grow.

The ideal pH for roses is a slightly acidic level of 6.0 to 6.8. Roses can tolerate pH down to 5.6, but will start to lose vigor when pH drops below that level. If the pH reading is below 6.0, lime should be added to the soil to raise it. The most effective limes are dolomitic and calcitic which can be applied at any time. Calcitic lime contains primarily calcium carbonate and little magnesium while dolomitic lime is a mix of both calcium and magnesium carbonates. Both types of lime will neutralize acidity, but dolomitic adds small amounts of magnesium to the soil and has a higher neutralization value. The rate of application is best determined by a soil test.

Rhode Island soils are young by geologic standards, having formed between 12,000 to 15,000 years ago from materials deposited from the last glacier. These soils are acidic due to the chemistry of the minerals in the bedrock from which they are derived. Plus, the high average annual rainfall (40 to 50 inches per year) has long ago washed calcium from the soil. Also, many types of mulch, farm manures, fertilizers, and other amendments that are added to improve soil are acidic in nature, which drives pH even lower. Since pH takes several months to change, we add lime to all our rose beds around Thanksgiving each year just before winterizing our gardens. We sprinkle it on with a trowel and let winter snow and rains wash it in. Once the pH level of the soil is correct, it is easy to maintain by checking it annually and adding a light application of lime when necessary.

> ## Testing pH
>
> pH can be tested by using pH strips or test meters, although inexpensive test meters are not always accurate. When test strips are used they are immersed in a mixture of soil and water (not distilled water, but the same water used to water roses) and a pH level is determined. The most accurate way to test soil and/or pH, however, is to send soil samples for professional testing. UMass Amherst has a Soil Testing Laboratory (413-545-2311) and other sources of testing can be found on-line.
>
> To prepare soil for professional testing, follow these simple steps, remembering to use clean equipment. Don't use brass or galvanized tools which can contaminate the soil samples. Also take samples when the soil is relatively dry. Since fertilizer or pesticide residue will skew the test results, the best time to take samples is in early spring.
>
> 1. Remove mulch or any organic material from the top of the soil.
> 2. Dig a hole 6" to 8" deep and shear off soil from the side of the hole, placing it into a clean plastic bucket.
> 3. Take 4-6 samples from different parts of the garden and mix the samples together.
> 4. Follow instructions for packaging and shipping the soil from the testing service.

Organic Amendments

Organic amendments are key ingredients to building first class soil. They originate from the remains of once-living materials and include compost, farm manures, seaweed, shredded bark, and leaf mold (decayed leaves and dead organisms). Some organic amendments have low nutrient content; others like compost are higher. All are excellent soil conditioners that hold water and nutrients, aerate and improve the tilth, or quality, of the soil, and buffer it against wide swings in pH. Organic amendments also feed beneficial microorganisms—bacteria, fungi, protozoa, and earthworms—that break down organic matter into nutrient forms that plants can absorb.

Adding organic amendments is a simple way of solving soil problems as well as improving soil. Just spread them on top of a rose bed, one to three inches thick, and then work them into the soil by hand or with a tiller. Organics can also be added to the backfill soil when planting. *(See Chapter 9: Planting)*

The primary organic material we use in our garden is horse manure. Horse manure is our manure of choice because it is readily available from local horse farms and has a pleasant stable odor that disappears in a day or two. All farm manures work better when aged six to twelve months, but we have used fresh horse manure when that's all we had, with no ill effects. Each fall we have two yards of it delivered from a nearby horse farm. We use it first as a winter cover and mulch, and then, when composted, add it to planting holes. Bags of composted or dehydrated manures or other packaged garden products provide smaller quantities of organic matter for the gardener with just a few plants.

Mulch

Applying one to three inches of mulch to rose beds has many advantages. Mulches insulate the soil in hot weather, help control weeds, conserve moisture in the soil, and enhance the overall appearance of the garden. The time to apply mulch is in late spring when the soil has warmed but before weeds have started to grow in earnest and before the real heat of summer has arrived. What mulch to use is a matter of personal choice, but there are two basic types, natural and synthetic.

Natural or organic mulches typically available in the New England area include compost, seaweed, woodchips, leaf mold, farm manures, pine bark, hemlock bark, and other commercially available products. Compost, seaweed, and leaf mold break down quickly and can be turned into the soil in the fall becoming soil amendments which add nutrients and improve soil structure. Others, like wood chips, are slow to decompose and deplete the soil of nitrogen. Determine what organic material is locally available and be creative. Try blending different types of mulches to create a distinctive soil cover that adds extra interest to your garden. We have blended chopped-up seaweed and horse manure together which makes a rich and unique topdressing out of locally available organics. Place groupings of quahog shells on the mulch and we have created a very distinctive seaside garden cover. What could be more New England than that?

Inorganic or synthetic mulches are water permeable landscape fabrics that are excellent in controlling weeds while allowing water and nutrients to pass through. These fabrics come in rolls of various sizes and can be purchased in many garden centers. Add a few inches of organic material on top and they become more functional and attractive.

Seaweed

Seaweed is "seafood" for roses. It is a multi-faceted resource that can be found in abundance in coastal New England. Not only can seaweed be used as a mulch, but as an effective soil conditioner and winter cover for roses.

Seaweed is a low-analysis fertilizer, more or less equivalent to that of farm manure. It is a teeming stew of micronutrients, hormones, vitamins, trace minerals, enzymes, amino acids, and growth stimulants, which can be taken up readily by plants. Seaweed contains all the macronutrients, major and minor, as well as some micronutrients, including manganese, iron, boron, zinc, copper, and mannitol, a simple sugar that makes micronutrients already in the soil available to plants.

Seaweed behaves like any other good mulch by conserving soil moisture and controlling weeds, but brings no weed seeds or plant diseases with it into the garden. It may also provide an added benefit in insect and disease control. In a study conducted by University of Rhode Island researchers, Neil Ross and Kathy Mallon, it was reported that seaweed usage may result in increased plant resistance to mites and aphids as well as some diseases, and possibly even to cold temperatures. ("Seaweed in the Home Garden," Rhode Island Sea Grant Fact Sheet, University of Rhode Island)

Seaweed is readily available for harvest. Believe it or not, the Rhode Island state constitution guarantees its citizens the right to gather seaweed from any public source, a throwback to the days when seaweed was an important agricultural resource. Just head to the beach with a rake and basket and help yourself. Almost any seaweed will do but do not remove any eelgrass growing on rocks because it is a protected species. On brisk January days we have gathered seaweed and, as a bonus, found large quahog shells which we used for garden decorations. We also have collected bags of seaweed at the home of a friend who lives on the shore on Buzzard's Bay where rows of seaweed resembling, in his words, "cassette tapes and lasagna pasta," piled up knee-deep at high tide.

Once we get home, we rinse out the fine beach sand as best we can. We could, at that point, mulch our rose beds freely with fresh seaweed without concern for salinity. Anecdotal evidence indicates no ill effects to the soil from salt with moderate seaweed use. We prefer to leave it in a pile for several weeks allowing rain to further rinse out sand before using it in the garden.

If seaweed collection is not an option, look for bags of seaweed and shellfish compost in garden centers. Seaweed concentrates, extracts, and liquid products that benefit roses can be found there, too.

Improving Soil

Rarely does perfect garden soil occur naturally. Gardeners can take soil as they find it and improve it by simply incorporating organics. Copious amounts of readily available organic matter can transform a dusty, worn out patch of earth into fertile garden soil in a matter of a season or two.

This re-birth of dead dirt into black gold is not complicated. We start off with soil as we find it and immediately improve it with aged manure and compost mixing these organics 50/50 with the existing soil. We add lime as a pH adjustor and turn over everything with a shovel and rototiller until the soil is uniform. If the organic amendments had been fresh, then we would have done this in the fall and allowed all the organic ingredients to settle in and decompose over the winter months and planted in the spring. Once fertile soil is established, it is easy to sustain its healthy composition by topdressing or mulching with organic material every spring. We constantly nourish the soil in our beds with a steady supply of horse manure every year, adding lime as necessary to maintain good pH.

Raised Beds

We like raised beds because we can control everything that goes into them, especially the soil composition. Raised beds provide excellent drainage, preventing waterlogged roots, and allow the soil to warm up sooner in the spring. Working in them reduces back strain and makes weeding easier. They can be configured in an endless array of shapes that improves landscape aesthetics on difficult sites.

Our mature rose garden consists of raised beds made from garden timbers or rocks and stones of various shapes and colors that we find add interest to our landscape. Some time ago, we visited friends in New Jersey and noticed a cache of red rocks excavated from a building site and slated to be thrown away. We loaded up the trunk and brought them home and built a small raised bed that we still use today. We have seen attractive and functional raised beds created from bricks, pavers, concrete blocks, redwood, cedar, and plastic composites that look like wood.

The raised beds in our garden are twelve inches high and four feet wide and as long as necessary. Four feet wide is an ideal width that makes it easy to reach in from either side to fertilize, prune, pull weeds or otherwise maintain rose bushes without stepping onto the garden soil, thus avoiding compaction. We have few rules in the garden but one of them is no stepping into the raised beds. This way the soil stays soft with lots of air spaces that allow water and air to penetrate all the way to the root zone. In irregular shaped beds, spots where stepping in is unavoidable, we have strategically placed flagstones used as stepping stones that can carry a person's weight without compressing the soil.

CHAPTER 5
STEP 3:
Plant in a Sunny Location

Roses need sunlight to grow and flower. Sunlight and the heat it brings are the environmental cues that start roses growing in April while diminishing sunlight triggers the slow onset of dormancy in late summer. Sun provides the solar energy that converts carbon dioxide in the atmosphere, along with water and minerals from the soil, into plant food through the remarkable process of photosynthesis.

How much daily sunshine do roses need? Six or more hours of direct continuous sunlight each day provides enough stimuli for full bloom production. While New England has a rich seaside tradition, there are a vast number of trees and forests everywhere. In fact, it is not easy to find any garden with uninterrupted dawn-to-dusk sunlight. In our shady Rhode Island garden a half-mile from the upper reaches of Narragansett Bay, sunlight is always at a premium.

Some varieties, however, tolerate less sunlight—even open shade—and the key is to identify them if sunshine is at a minimum. In general, varieties with fewer petals in their blooms do well enough on less than six hours of sunlight. For instance, the white floribunda 'Iceberg', with eighteen to twenty petals, blooms nicely in our rose garden in the fall on less than four hours of sunlight.

Morning sunlight is considered somewhat better than afternoon because it dries dew and any overnight moisture on foliage, preventing the spread of fungal diseases. Plus it is less likely to singe leaves and blooms than scorching mid-summer afternoon sun. However, if roses have spindly, leggy canes, stems spaced further apart than normal, meager flower production, and a general loss of vigor, they are planted in too much shade and need to be moved.

If a garden is located in an area that gets less than six hours of sunlight, one solution is to grow roses in containers. Containerized roses can be moved from place to place, gaining additional sun exposure which is one reason why we grow many of our roses in containers. We can slow down the bloom cycle by moving them into the shade or accelerate it by placing them in a sunnier location.

Can there be too much sunshine? Not in early summer. But later in the season, sunshine brings intense heat. Historically the hottest period of the year in New England is late July through early August when daily temperatures may rise above 90°F. When it gets this hot, rose blooms are smaller, petals burn on many varieties, and colors fade. But roses are tough plants and will easily survive hot weather with extra watering during these annual heat waves.

By late August, cooler temperatures and a few drenching rains jump-start roses that had hunkered down during mid-summer heat. The autumn bloom cycle features more intense colors uniquely different from the June bloom. Some whites turn a little pink, and bi-color roses show sharper contrasts. 'Playboy', a scarlet and gold floribunda, and 'Double Delight', a hybrid tea with a stunning blend of red and white, display their colors with different intensities depending on the amount of sunlight they receive. Autumn roses are special and, with enough sunlight and the absence of an early hard frost, it is possible to have fresh roses from your garden on your Thanksgiving table.

Microclimates

New England has striking variations of geography that influence the plants growing here. The six-state area has thousands of miles of jagged Atlantic coastline including large bays and harbors, intimate coves and countless inlets. Inland, New England has lakes and valleys together with rocky hills and mountains at higher elevations. This wide range of topography has a profound influence on the climate and weather.

Local conditions also have a significant impact on climate. These microclimates occur when local conditions differ from the area surrounding it. These differing conditions may be no more than pockets that may be warmer or colder, have more shade, or be wetter or windier. Different microclimates can occur in the same cities and towns, the same neighborhoods, on the same property, even on different sides of the same house. A rose garden planted with a southern exposure against a white structure in full daily sun will perform completely differently than the same roses planted in a bed on the opposite side of the same house with shade trees close by. These areas may be small but the differences can be significant.

The Victorian Rose Garden in Roger Williams Park in Providence, RI, for instance, with dawn-to-dusk sunshine, blooms five to ten days earlier than our much cooler East Providence garden only eight miles away. The forsythia blooms a week earlier in warmer Pawtucket, the next city north of us and a few miles further away from the cooling effects of Narragansett Bay.

We removed two large maple trees from our front yard several years ago which completely changed the plant dynamics in our front garden. This garden, with many roses of the same varieties as our shadier backyard garden, now has direct sunlight from dawn through mid-afternoon and the differences are amazing. The roses grow fuller and faster, have more flowers of sharper color, and bloom much later into the fall. However, we also found that certain mauve varieties that grew very well in our cooler backyard garden did not tolerate the additional heat now present in the new garden. The blooms of 'Rhapsody in Blue', a lovely purple shrub rose, literally shattered and fell apart with the first heat of the season.

These natural environmental conditions that create microclimates can be dramatic and must be taken into consideration when selecting planting sites and the rose varieties that will have to grow there.

CHAPTER 6

STEP 4:
Provide Plenty of Water

Roses need water. They require frequent watering as long as they are actively growing and in most of New England, that is from mid-April through October.

Water plays a major role in photosynthesis. It also transports nutrients from the root zone throughout the plant and cools roses through transpiration, the process by which water evaporates through the leaves. Water keeps plant cells turgid—full of water—and provides both strength and substance to the blooms and foliage.

Since roses are flowering shrubs with large root systems, they need a deep watering that soaks all the way down into the root zone several times a week. How much water is enough? Many suggest an inch per plant per week, but what exactly is an inch per week? A mathematician can convert inches of water into gallons depending on the area that is being watered, but his calculations do not include other factors such as soil type, temperature, and humidity. Our advice is simply to measure water in gallons. For a medium sized, mature plant this can range anywhere from five gallons per plant per week to double that when it is hot and dry. Of course, apply less for smaller roses and more for larger roses.

Keep in mind that the "inch per week" or the five-gallon per week answer is impacted by a host of environmental factors which influence the amount of water roses require. Are they planted in full sun or partial shade? Are they in an area where there is reflected heat or light from a nearby building or fence? Roses in a sunny, southern exposure need more water than those in a cooler, shadier location. Roses planted in an open, windy area need more water than those planted in a protected location because wind dries out both the soil and plant. To make this more interesting, all of these conditions can and will vary from one garden to the next according to individual microclimates.

Fluctuations in the weather also influence the watering schedule. When the temperature goes beyond 90 degrees, roses may need to be watered every day. The watering schedule can be adjusted during periods of deep, soaking rain, but sometimes even rainy days may not provide enough water to penetrate to the roots.

Another variable is the composition of the garden soil. Coastal New England soil, for instance, is mainly sandy loam and drains well. Some areas of Connecticut have clay soil which holds water and drains slowly. Check to see what happens when water is applied to your garden soil. See how long it takes the water to be absorbed and if it takes more than a few minutes, there may be a drainage problem. If the soil is too sandy and drains too quickly, add organics. If the garden soil smells boggy, there is definitely a drainage problem and rose roots will soon rot in soil that remains perpetually soaked in water. If this is the case and the waterlogged soil cannot be amended to properly drain, then abandon the site for rose cultivation.

Deciding when roses need water can be determined by using a fool proof, low-tech test. Push your thumb into the soil at the base of each plant and check for moisture: if it feels dry, then add water. If in doubt, add water. The key is to keep the soil moist all the time. Remember that water has to percolate down into the root zone, twelve to eighteen inches, to be effective. Watering heavily, two or three times each week, is more beneficial than a light watering every day, especially in mid-summer heat. In cool weather, once or twice per week is sufficient. Applying two inches of mulch goes a long way towards conserving water and preventing evaporation.

How to Water

Traditionally, water is applied to the soil at the base of the rose, which keeps the foliage dry and avoids spreading water-born fungal diseases. This can be done simply by using a hand-held water wand or employing various irrigation systems. Building a well with soil several inches high around the base of each rose—creating a reservoir—makes watering more efficient no matter what method you use.

Hand watering can be time consuming, depending on the number of roses, but if time is not an issue, it is a good way to observe your plants on a regular basis. It gives you an opportunity to look for signs of new growth and bud development as well as diseases or insect damage. Fill each well with water, let drain and fill up again, repeating two or three times to provide a deep soaking. Use a gentle stream, not a hard spray, to keep water from splashing up onto the foliage which encourages fungal diseases like blackspot.

Drip-irrigation is an easy-to-install, effective alternative to hand watering, especially with larger gardens. Aboveground emitters are placed at the base of each rose that gently discharge water. The emitters are fed through narrow tubes that distribute water evenly to each plant. These tubes lie on top of the soil or can be covered by mulch. How long you need to run your irrigation depends on the water pressure available. Measure this by placing an emitter into a five-gallon bucket and time how long it takes to fill. It took one hour with the water pressure in our garden and now we know how long it takes to supply five gallons of water to each rose bush. In hot weather, we let the system run for an hour; in cooler weather we decrease the time. When using this type of irrigation system check occasionally to be sure the emitters are working because the narrow tubes can clog from time to time. Check the soil frequently and adjust the irrigation schedule to avoid dry soil.

Soaker hoses exude or "sweat" water through tiny pores in the hoses. The disadvantage of soaker hoses is that they may distribute water unevenly, releasing more water at the beginning of the hose and less at the end. They can also clog and if the hoses are buried in mulch, the clogged hoses may go unnoticed.

Overhead sprinklers can be used occasionally to clean foliage, wash off aphids and spider mites, plus cool roses in hot weather. A disadvantage here is that overhead watering wets the foliage for long periods of time encouraging blackspot and the increasing humidity causes powdery mildew. The rain-like effect of overhead sprinklers may also make blooms and buds of some varieties soggy, causing them to ball up and not open. Finally, minerals in the water sometimes leave unattractive spots on the foliage when dried. The best time to use overhead sprinklers, if at all, is in the early morning so the foliage can dry quickly.

Watering Container Roses

Roses planted in pots or decorative containers need to be watered more frequently than roses planted in the ground because the soil in containers dries out much more quickly. Roses planted in dark colored pots absorb more heat and dry out even faster than those planted in lighter colored containers. To avoid waterlogged roots when planting roses directly in decorative containers, make certain the containers have drainage holes. When double potting roses—placing plastic pots into decorative containers—check to be sure that both containers have drainage holes. Don't let water sit in either container.

Polymers: An Aid to Watering

A great aid in maintaining moisture in both containers and rose beds are water crystals or polymers. These polymers (brand names like *Soil Moist* and *P-4*) are non-toxic and look like sea salt when dry, but when hydrated, they will soften and grow many times their size as they absorb water. Water crystals can lessen the amount of watering needed since as the soil dries out, they release the water they retain back into the soil. In addition to reducing the amount of watering they also improve soil aeration by the constant action of their expansion and contraction.

Pre-hydrate polymers before using, but be careful; a small handful dissolved in a couple of gallons of water will expand and fill the container with finished product. Start with a large container and check the label for the recommended ratio of water to crystals. Hydrate them overnight and they will expand into a soft, jello-like substance which then can be mixed into the potting soil. Hydrated crystals can also be put into the planting hole. Just remember to use hydrated polymers. Gardeners have been known to throw dry polymers into the planting hole only to find, after the first soaking rain, their roses have been literally uprooted when the polymers expanded.

Rainwater

Since roses need plenty of water, take advantage of a free renewable resource—rainwater. Rainwater is warm, soft, chlorine-free water—free of minerals, salts, pesticides and other contaminants that ground water eventually collects from soil. Harvesting rainwater is an ecologically sound way of augmenting tap water and has other advantages as well. It reduces pollution of surface water, helps to control flooding, lessens demands on the local water supply and, best of all, saves money by reducing water bills. All it takes is a barrel placed under a downspout.

Any large, clean barrel can be turned into an effective rain barrel or a barrel can be purchased ready-to-go, full of accessories. Customized rain barrels feature screw-on tops with screen mesh filters, overflow valves, hose connections, brass spigots and drain plugs.

You can ladle rainwater out of the barrel by hand if you have only a few plants or hook your barrel up to a drip irrigation system. If the distance the rainwater in the barrel has to travel is more than a few feet, installing a small water pump will increase water pressure.

Watering Tips

In addition to watering established roses, keep in mind that water is especially important when planting, transplanting and fertilizing roses. Here are some watering tips to remember:

- Newly planted roses require more water because their root systems are not yet established. Under-watering results in shallow root systems which will dry out more quickly.

- Water transplanted roses well to reestablish their roots.

- Blooming roses need more water than roses out of bloom because water is lost through petals and leaves. Wilting blooms are a symptom of inadequate water.

- Water roses in the fall before the ground freezes but before adding winter protection. Once the ground freezes, roots are unable to absorb water. Well-watered roses have a much better chance of surviving winter stresses and suffer less winter kill.

- Always water your roses heavily before spraying with pesticides to avoid damage to the foliage and blooms.

- Water roses before fertilizing to avoid burning roots and foliage.

CHAPTER 7

STEP 5:
Fertilize Frequently

Roses, like people, need food and water served up on a regular basis to be healthy and realize their full growth potential. Roses eat and drink their way through nutrients all season. These nutrients should be in the soil when roses are actively growing and must be replenished regularly.

Types of Nutrients

The major categories of nutrients are *macronutrients*—composed of major and minor nutrients—and *micronutrients*. The most common nutrients, needed in the largest quantities, are major nutrients and the most important of these are nitrogen (N), phosphorous (P), and potassium (K).

- **Nitrogen** fuels the growth of roses and is the element that they need the most. It stimulates the development of tall canes, healthy blooms, and dark foliage. Nitrogen can move rapidly, depending on its form, through the soil and should be replenished throughout the growing season.

- **Phosphorous** encourages root growth which leads to healthy flower production and is necessary for photosynthesis. This element moves through the soil very slowly and should be added to the soil at the time of planting.

- **Potassium** helps regulate the metabolism of the plant, encourages root growth, vigor, and bloom color, as well as disease resistance. It regulates water use and moderates the effects of nitrogen and phosphorous.

In addition to these major nutrients, there are a host of other elements—minor nutrients and micronutrients—that are essential to roses, but only in small quantities. The minor nutrients are calcium, magnesium, sulfur and iron; the micronutrients include manganese, copper, zinc, boron, molybdenum, and chlorine. Many of these are already present in sufficient amounts in the soil, air, or water. Calcium, magnesium, sulfur, and iron may need to be added to the soil from time to time, but only if necessary. An occasional soil test can determine any nutrient deficiency.

Types of Fertilizers

Feeding roses the nutrients they need can be accomplished easily with fertilizers purchased at nurseries and garden centers. They come in different forms including granules, powders, or liquids and are classified as either inorganic or organic. Both types have advantages.

Inorganic or chemical fertilizers contain no organic material. They are synthetic products made from mineral salts and deliver key nutrients in sufficient quantities quickly. These inexpensive commercial fertilizers indicate the percentage of the three most needed macronutrients—nitrogen, phosphorous, and potassium (N-P-K) in that order—on the label. This is referred to as the NPK ratio. A balanced fertilizer of 10-10-10 is a good general mix for roses: 10 percent nitrogen, 10 percent phosphorous, 10 percent potassium. Some formulations also may include micronutrients which will be listed on the label.

Organic fertilizers are measured blends of natural animal or vegetable byproducts like blood meal, cottonseed meal, and bone meal as well as kelp and fish emulsion that feed plants while building the soil. Organic fertilizers depend on microorganisms in the soil to break them down into forms that plants can absorb. This release of nutrients occurs over a longer period of time than the equivalent amount of synthetic fertilizers. Organic products perform other functions, too. They allow soil to hold more water, improve soil structure, and increase bacterial activity.

Water-soluble products come as solid or liquid concentrates and when mixed with water are usually applied as a soil drench. Some can be utilized as a foliar feed, too, because leaves can absorb certain nutrients faster than roots can. Double check the label to be certain that the fertilizer you have can be used on foliage. Follow the instructions since careless foliar feeding can burn leaves. Water soluble fertilizers are fast acting and often contain micronutrients absent from granular fertilizers.

Slow release fertilizers look like little capsules or pellets with a special coating that release nutrients over long periods of time. This slow release action reduces the chances of fertilizer burn. Look for a formulation that releases over a three or four month period and apply in late April or early May. Longer release times or later application may stimulate unwanted growth into the autumn at a time when roses should be slowly slipping towards dormancy.

Roses can't tell the difference between sources of nutrients since essential nutrients are the same regardless of where they come from. Nutrients from a bag of synthetic 10-10-10 are the same as the nutrients present in a bag of blended organic fertilizer. However, different types of fertilizers have side effects that can affect plants in various ways. For example, the organic fertilizer slowly releases its nutrients into the soil while the chemical fertilizers are accurately measured concentrations of selected elements that are ready for immediate uptake.

Which is the better choice? We like the consistency and relatively quick uptake of synthetic fertilizers not to mention its ready availability and reasonable cost. But if only synthetic fertilizers are used, the soil eventually loses its organic matter and the ability to hold water. We use both types of fertilizers in our gardens. Monthly feedings of 10-10-10 are augmented with fish emulsion and seaweed extract, great organic sources of nutrients. This, along with plenty of organic amendments, replenishes the organic matter in the soil.

> **Types of Nutrients**
>
> 1. Macronutrients
>   A. Major Nutrients:
>   Nitrogen
>   Phosphorous
>   Potassium
>   B. Minor Nutrients:
>   Calcium
>   Iron
>   Magnesium
>   Sulfur
> 2. Micronutrients
>   Boron
>   Chlorine
>   Copper
>   Manganese
>   Molybdenum
>   Zinc

Fertilizing Program

Roses are hungry plants and need to be fertilized more than once per season. They thrive when fertilized regularly with either chemical or organic fertilizers (or both) that deliver key nutrients in sufficient amounts. The best way to accomplish a steady flow of nutrients is to develop a fertilization program with scheduled feedings during the growing season. Our program is a mix of chemical and organic fertilizers, plus plenty of water, supplemented with occasional applications of water-soluble products. This is a simple, economical system that maintains an even stream of essential nutrients to our roses all summer.

When to Fertilize

It does no good to apply fertilizer on cold, dormant soil. The microorganisms in the soil are dormant, too, and not able to break down organic matter and release nutrients before the fertilizer is washed away. We wait until the very end of April or early May to apply the first feeding of the season.

Plant growth in early spring is initially triggered by increasing daylight and heat from solar radiation, causing air temperatures to rise. This rising air temperature stimulates buds to swell and break into new stems, supported for a short time by energy stored in canes and roots from the previous season. As soil temperatures rise, the microorganisms in the soil awaken from dormancy and begin processing organic matter, releasing nutrients that roses absorb through their roots. These nutrients in the soil start to release when the soil temperature reaches approximately 40°F and continue to release more nutrients as the soil gets warmer. The annual explosion of bright yellow forsythia blossoms in early spring is a sure sign that the soil has warmed to about 55°F which is sufficient to support growth.

Fertilize roses for the first time after spring pruning and when there is an inch or two of new growth. In southern New England this is mid to late April—certainly by May first.

The second feeding should be given after the first flush or bloom cycle goes by in late June or early July. Fertilize for the third time in early August, about two months prior to the first frost.

This program of fertilizing three times during the growing season provides enough nutrients to grow very good roses. But you can go one better with a gourmet program of four feedings. The "meal plan" in our garden includes a balanced, granular mix of synthetic 10-10-10 or an equivalent organic fertilizer four times each season, May through August, applied on the first weekend of each month. This granular fertilizer is our primary source of nutrients—think of it

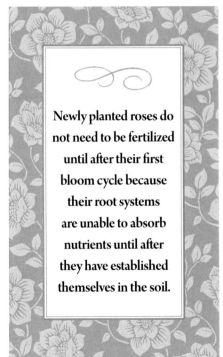

Newly planted roses do not need to be fertilized until after their first bloom cycle because their root systems are unable to absorb nutrients until after they have established themselves in the soil.

as meat and potatoes. It stays in the soil, feeding the plants until the next application.

We supplement these feedings with occasional applications of fast acting water-soluble fertilizers in between dry feedings. The water-soluble product that we use contains the micronutrients that roses require in small amounts—think of this as dessert. In addition, we like to experiment with new and different nutrient sources, especially if they are organic. We have tried various fish emulsions and seaweed extracts plus an interesting organic tonic that included bat guano. We found that these products were all beneficial to roses when used according to the dosages and instructions on the label.

Add copious amounts of water to this feeding schedule, and we have a continuous stream of nutrients and water all season long. The results are beautiful roses.

How Much to Apply

Always read the product label and follow the recommended application rate and other instructions. A good guideline for four monthly feedings is to apply one-third cup of granular 10-10-10 to each well-established, mid-sized hybrid tea or floribunda at each application. Since big roses need more fertilizer, fertilize larger roses—like climbers, mature old garden roses, and shrub roses—more than hybrid teas and floribundas. Fertilize miniature roses with half of what is given to hybrid teas. Don't overdo it. If you see that the foliage turns crispy and brown soon after fertilizing, it may indicate too much fertilizer on dry plants. If this is the case, flood the soil with water immediately, flushing the excess nutrients away. Another indication of over fertilizing is excessively large foliage out of proportion to the stems and flowers.

How to Fertilize Using Granular or Dry Fertilizers

- First water the soil well before fertilizing to prevent root burn.
- Next pull away any mulch from the base of the plant and apply granular or other dry fertilizers around the drip line, the imaginary circle formed under the outermost leaves of the rose. Keep the fertilizer away from the bud union, or crown, in the center of the plant.
- Then lightly scratch the fertilizer in with a hand tool and water well again. Remember that nutrients must be in solution and washed into the root zone before roses are able to absorb them. When fertilizing and watering is done, push the mulch back into place.

When using water-soluble fertilizers, mix them in containers large enough to hold three to five gallons of liquid or whatever size you can safely lift and carry. Monthly dosages for liquid fertilizers are usually measured as so many teaspoons or tablespoons per gallon and so many gallons per rose bush. This information will be on the label. Once mixed, liquid fertilizers can either be ladled out by hand or applied with siphon hoses to the soil at the base of the plant.

We used to dole out liquid fertilizer by hand using an old plastic one gallon milk jug. As our garden grew, this became too much work and now, when we apply it to our garden roses, we add it to the irrigation system—fertilizing and watering at the same time. When we fertilize our container roses, we use liquid fertilizers only. Because liquids wash through the potting soil into the root zone immediately, it is absorbed by the plant quickly. This is good. But much of it drips through the drainage holes out of the container just as quickly. This is bad. We solved this problem by cutting the dosage in quarters and applying weekly, thus establishing a constant level of nutrients without wasting any.

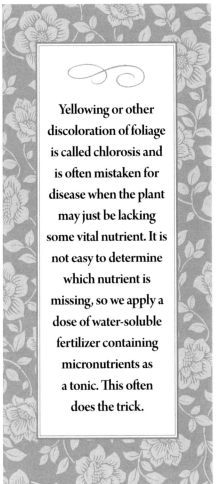

Yellowing or other discoloration of foliage is called chlorosis and is often mistaken for disease when the plant may just be lacking some vital nutrient. It is not easy to determine which nutrient is missing, so we apply a dose of water-soluble fertilizer containing micronutrients as a tonic. This often does the trick.

Keep in mind that most New England soils are acidic in nature and nutrient availability is influenced by the acidity (pH) of the soil. If the pH is lower than 5.6, the nutrients begin to react with each other forming insoluble compounds and are said to be "locked-up" in the soil—unavailable for absorption by the rose's roots. It is possible for roses to become malnourished even with ample nutrients present in the soil if the pH is too low.

CHAPTER 8

STEP 6:
Managing Insects & Diseases

Managing insects and diseases does not have to take the enjoyment out of rose gardening. Many gardeners are bewildered by the complexities surrounding insects and diseases. They are unable to separate good bugs from bad and become discouraged when common rose diseases arrive seemingly out of nowhere. Half the battle is realizing that these problems exist; the other half is discovering the various effective insect and disease remedies available. Once you decide on the degree of tolerance you have for garden pests, it becomes easier to choose what kind of pest management is best for you and your garden.

Integrated Pest Management (IPM) is the method used to determine whether to treat, when to treat, and how to treat garden insects and diseases. It is a process that measures how much tolerance a rose gardener has for rose pests while selecting the least harmful means to achieve the desired result. This decision will vary from gardener to gardener. A casual rose gardener may accept a certain level of damage from pests while a more intense gardener may demand spotless conditions. Most of us fall somewhere in between. Regardless of what your tolerance level is, there are four basic choices available when dealing with rose insects and diseases: planting varieties that have a demonstrated resistance to common rose diseases; employing organic gardening practices; using chemical products; and a combination of the three.

Plant Sustainable Varieties

The first option that rose gardeners have is selecting sustainable varieties. These varieties, if they are not species roses, are products of breeding programs where disease resistance is a principal hybridizing objective. One way to identify sustainable rose varieties is to visit public rose gardens where insect and disease controls may be marginal or nonexistent. The June bloom may be stunning and show very little evidence of rose disease and insect problems, but another visit in mid-summer will make apparent which varieties are prone to insects and diseases.

In addition to tried and true disease resistant varieties, such as rugosa roses and many varieties of shrubs and old garden roses, the selection of modern, easy care, disease resistant varieties is growing larger. The rose industry recognizes the public's increasing demand for low maintenance roses and ranks cleanliness and disease resistance as important characteristics in their evaluations of new varieties.

Every year new varieties are being introduced that have been bred specifically for their disease resistance. The immaculate modern shrub rose 'Knock Out', for instance, is the gold standard for cleanliness and, if you like pink roses, 'Pretty Lady', a small floribunda with a cast iron constitution, is a good choice. 'Home Run', introduced in 2006, has bright red blooms and is nearly as disease resistant as 'Knock Out', one of its parents. While there are no roses that are totally immune to insect damage and disease, there are more disease resistant varieties available than you think. New resistant varieties are being introduced every year, providing additional choices. *(See list of sustainable varieties in Chapter 12.)*

Organic Option

The second option in controlling garden pests is to maintain an organic garden. Organic gardening consists of using good horticultural practices, which include maintaining a clean garden and providing a healthy environment. Giving roses what they need—sunlight, water, fertilizer and good soil—leads to healthy plants. Healthy plants have strong immune systems that enable them to survive bouts with insects and diseases.

The importance of adding organics to the soil and maintaining proper pH should not be underestimated. Roses grown in poor soil and not given enough nutrients become weak and stressed. They are more likely to succumb to damage created by garden pests, not because they were necessarily frail varieties, but because they lacked the benefits of basic rose care. Even the best disease resistant varieties can fail to thrive when neglected.

Providing air circulation within the plant by opening up its center through careful pruning, planting roses far enough apart to prevent overcrowding, and keeping foliage dry when watering are all good gardening practices. Keep your garden clean by pruning off diseased canes, picking up diseased foliage lying in your rose beds, and discarding it all in the trash. Do not add any diseased plant material to a compost pile. Taking these steps goes a long way towards keeping your roses free from fungal diseases.

Organic sprays, including some potassium bicarbonate-based fungicides, can be used to keep diseases under control, but remember that most fungicides, including organic ones, are not a cure. They can control diseases and prevent them from spreading, but will not eradicate them. Some insecticidal soaps and other sprays may have some level of control against insects and diseases, but they can still damage plants if not used properly. Use them with caution and always read the label.

Adding diversity in your garden by planting other plant species—companion planting—is another way of providing roses with a friendly, healthy environment. Minimize the presence of harmful insects by planting flowers that attract beneficial insects. This will help keep harmful insects in check. Good companions to roses include garlic, alyssum, thyme, oregano, chives, scented geraniums, marigolds, lavender, dwarf sunflowers and daylilies. When beneficial insects are attracted to your garden, they settle in and perpetuate their numbers by feeding upon the bad bugs thus helping to reduce damage.

Some destructive insects can be controlled with no harm to the environment. Insects like aphids and spider mites can be washed off with blasts of water, but spider mites have been known to crawl back up roses. Plus their reproductive cycle is every three days. It makes sense, then, to apply this water treatment every three days for a couple of weeks or until the mites are completely frustrated. We used to have an awful infestation of spider mites in our garden that began in early July when the weather turned hot. Insecticides had no effect on them. We controlled them to some degree with water treatments, but it wasn't until we eliminated insecticide usage that the spider mite problem went away by itself within a few seasons. We surmised that insect predators of spider mites retuned to our garden as beneficial bugs when it was safe for them to do so.

Japanese beetles can be removed by handpicking them off the plant and disposing of them in a container of water. When the container is full, just toss the solution of dead beetles onto the grass and let the birds finish the job. The best long-term solution to Japanese beetles, though, is to attack them in their larvae (grub) stage in the soil. Apply milky spore or other organic lawn care products designed for this purpose at the right time in late spring or late summer when the grubs are vulnerable.

Birds are natural predators of many harmful insects and can be easily attracted by setting up a birdbath or hanging feeders in or near the garden—one more way to maintain a healthy balance between good bugs and bad. Constantly monitor and observe your garden and be aware of problems as they occur. Logging garden events into a garden journal from season to season keeps track of your garden's progress and its problems. A journal will provide a timetable of when certain insects and diseases appeared as well as a record of what controls you used in the past and if they were successful.

Chemical Option

The third option for those gardeners who find that using organic methods does not give them a high enough level of control over garden pests is to use chemical pesticides. Effective pesticides labeled for roses and for use in the home garden can be found in nurseries and garden centers. They are sold as insecticides, fungicides, miticides, or combinations of the three. When used as directed and at the recommended dosage, they will successfully control garden insects and diseases.

To control insects, wait until you see them or the damage they cause before applying insecticides. Use insecticides only when needed and apply only enough to eliminate the pests. It is not necessary to add insecticides to the spray mix at every application of your spray program. Keep in mind that broad-spectrum insecticides do not discriminate between good and bad bugs. They destroy them all, offsetting whatever balance existed between them. Fungicides, on the other hand, must be applied preemptively and used continuously all season because fungi spores are present on the plant long before the damage they cause becomes noticeable.

Always hydrate plants prior to the application of any spray material whether it is organic or non-organic. Burnt foliage and other serious damage can result by applying any spray material to dry plants. Never apply pesticides of any kind to rugosa roses at any time; their foliage is easily damaged. Check labels for the temperature range recommended and spray during the coolest part of the day, either in early morning or evening. Avoid spraying in direct sunlight on a hot day and, it goes without saying, never spray in windy weather. Always follow directions on the label and use protection. When using chemical sprays, follow proper spraying techniques and use safety equipment such as goggles, respirator and gloves as well as protective clothing to prevent dermal absorption of spray material.

If you choose this option, be aware that the list of garden pesticides labeled for use in home gardens is steadily growing shorter and becoming more expensive. Eventually this will make the use of chemical pesticides as the sole approach to insect and disease control the least desirable choice.

Combined Approach

The final option of dealing with garden insects and diseases is a combination of the first three choices. In our garden, we are moving from high maintenance rose varieties to a garden of disease resistant roses. We make sure our roses are well watered and fed regularly. We prune out diseased canes and foliage, pick off Japanese beetles by hand, and use blasts of water to rid the garden of spider mites and aphids. We supplement this with a scaled down spray program using modern, less toxic fungicides. We also keep an eye out for new developments in biotechnology that will further reduce the need for pesticides. By replanting our garden, rose-by-rose, with sustainable varieties, mostly modern shrubs and floribundas, we hope to eventually eliminate chemical sprays altogether.

> **Choices for Controlling Insects & Diseases**
>
> 1. Plant sustainable varieties
> 2. Use organic option
> 3. Use chemical option
> 4. Use combined approach

The best defense against disease and insect damage is maintaining strong, healthy roses right from the start. This includes choosing the right varieties for your garden; proper planting in rich, organic, well-drained soil; timely pruning of diseased and damaged canes; and supplying plenty of food and water on a regular basis. Although any rose can suffer damage from garden pests, healthy plants have tougher immune systems and are far more able to survive these attacks.

Insects

It helps to recognize the difference between beneficial garden insects and destructive ones that are likely to inhabit a New England garden. Not every insect is undesirable. In fact, there is an army of beneficial insects working quietly behind the scenes serving as natural biological controls, limiting the damage from bad bugs. These good bugs prey on common harmful insects, thus establishing somewhat of a balance in the insect population. While some beneficial insects will also snack on other beneficial insects, in general roses will benefit from this rough entomological harmony.

Some of these predaceous insects are easy to see, but most work silently in the shadows and it takes a keen eye to spot them. The good bugs will remain in a garden as long as they have a food source. We see ladybugs all the time and know what voracious appetites they have for aphids. Green lacewing adults and larvae also like aphids, and will dine on small caterpillars, too. Tiny spiders that live in mulch and ground litter are not so obvious but they are the number one predator of insects even though they are arachnids, not even insects at all. Some spin webs to trap their meals and others hunt prey on the ground or crawl around in plants.

The next time you see a large black beetle scurrying out from under a log or garden mulch, try not to bash it with your weeder. It's probably a ground beetle that eats grubs, ant eggs, cut worms or anything else that spends part of its life cycle on the ground.

Dragonflies eat mosquitoes; praying mantis grab insects with their modified front legs; and even yellow jackets, when not dive bombing on your picnic lunch, eat caterpillars, flies, and beetle grubs. Add a frog or toad softly hopping along looking for a tasty bug to eat and a rose garden becomes a hostile and dangerous place for an unlucky insect.

No matter how many good bugs we are lucky enough to have in our gardens, it is the presence of bad insects that we notice the most. Some well-known destructive insects, like aphids and Japanese beetles, are familiar and easy to identify. Others are so small or secretive that they can only be recognized by the damage they cause. Blind shoots, stems that terminate with neither a bud nor a bloom, may indicate the presence of the tiny rose midge and the telltale hole in the pith of a cane is a sure sign of cane borers. The first indication of the pesty two-spotted spider mite is the lower foliage turning yellow and small salt and pepper spots appearing on the undersides of the leaves. Look closely and tiny webs may be evident.

Amid all this entomological activity, we have discovered some interesting creatures living in our garden that are sometimes easy to overlook. Leafrollers, for instance, lay eggs on rose leaves then carefully roll them up, like a rug, with the eggs inside, all held together with webbing. The emerging larvae feed on the leaves causing some foliage damage. Sometimes we unroll the leaves out of curiosity, but usually we just pluck the leaf off and discard it. Spittle bugs are another odd resident of the garden. These tiny green insects whip up a foamy mass of bubbles on a stem and then hide inside the "spittle." They can be easily rubbed off with a flick of a finger or with a blast of water from the hose.

Every season without fail, we find holes drilled into the cross section of freshly pruned canes by cane borers, small wasps that are so sneaky that we have never, ever seen them at work. While these insects are more of a novelty than a nuisance, we have other less desirable creepy-crawlies lurking in the garden. Asiatic beetles are chestnut brown bugs about a half-inch long that hunker down in the soil during the day and slip out at night to feed on vegetation, including roses. They have a life cycle similar to that of Japanese beetles and generally arrive in July for four or five weeks. Like Japanese beetles, the best long-range controls for Asiatic beetles are timely soil treatments aimed at their larvae (grub) stage of development. Several effective products designed to eliminate insects in the soil can be found at garden centers.

Garden troublemakers are not limited to insects but include small animals. We had a family of chipmunks move in one summer and dig their little holes in the rose garden. We stomped soil into one hole only to find it nicely cleaned out the following morning. When we tried jamming a stone into the same hole, another hole popped up next to it a few hours later. This quickly turned into a fool's errand and we surrendered, outsmarted by Chip and Dale.

There is such an incredible diversity of insects in even a small rose garden that observing them and sorting out the differences between them can become another way to enjoy rose gardening.

Insects: Symptoms & Controls

Some of the common rose insects likely to appear in New England rose gardens include aphids, cane borers, midge, thrips, spider mites, and Japanese beetles.

Aphids, tiny green or black bugs about 1/8-inch long, are very common rose insects, attracted by the nitrogen present in new growth and buds. They appear mainly during the spring and quickly multiply during warm weather. Aphids suck the sap from the plant and excrete a sweet, sticky substance called honeydew which attracts ants.

Symptoms: Aphids draw out plant juices from the tender parts of the plant—new foliage, buds, and peduncles are the most vulnerable. The honeydew excreted by these insects is sticky and encourages the growth of black, sooty mold.

Solutions: Aphids can be knocked off the plant by forcefully spraying them with water. Natural enemies of aphids include lady beetles and lacewing larvae. Plants that may repel aphids include garlic, dill, catnip and marigolds. Plant yarrow to attract ladybugs which are natural predators of aphids. Spraying with an insecticidal soap or a chemical insecticide are other options. Never spray rugosa roses because their foliage is easily damaged by chemical pesticides.

Cane Borers are small wasps and bees that bore a hole in the pith or crosscut of a freshly pruned cane where they build their nests.

Symptoms: A hole in the middle of a cane is easily noticeable and may be a few inches down or all the way to the crown of the rose bush.

Solutions: Most cane borers feed on aphids, so if aphids are kept under control, so are cane borers. Infested canes should be cut below the level of the nest and discarded. Another solution is to seal each freshly cut cane with waterproof wood glue before cane borers can bore a hole, but the glue can be unattractive (try *Elmer's Glue* which dries clear) and many gardeners just choose to prune off the affected canes.

Midges are tiny, almost invisible insects. The adult lays eggs on new growth and under the sepals of flower buds. The eggs hatch in two days and feed on the new growth, causing it to die. This prevents the development of buds. When midges reach maturity in a week's time, they fall off the plant to the ground where they pupate in tiny cocoons. New adults emerge in three to seven days and the cycle repeats.

Symptoms: The rose bush looks healthy but does not produce flowers. A small crisp, burnt-like bit of foliage at the tip of the new growth may appear. A stem that terminates without a bud or bloom is called a blind shoot. (Not all blind shoots are caused by midges but may be due to environmental factors.) A garden infested with midges will have few blooms.

Solutions: In early spring inspect plants every week to check for midges. The blind shoots should be pruned out and discarded as they appear. Heavily scented herbs and alliums may discourage an infestation. Spraying with an insecticide is another option. Never spray rugosa roses because their foliage is easily damaged by chemical pesticides.

Spittle Bugs are small, green, beetle-shaped insects that usually appear in early spring during the first bloom cycle.

Symptoms: White, frothy foam appears on new stems. The spittle bugs are inside this foam.

Solutions: Use a strong spray of water to remove the foam and bugs which can also be picked off by hand and destroyed.

Thrips are tiny, brownish insects with yellow wings. They feed on the petals of rose buds and blooms, often preferring light-colored roses.

Symptoms: An infestation of thrips will result in deformed buds, buds that have brown edges, or buds that do not open. Spots or streaks on open blooms may also indicate thrips. On close examination, these small insects can be seen hiding inside the flower.

Solutions: Lacewing larvae feed on thrips. Planting alliums may act as a deterrent. A solution for controlling thrips is to spray the blooms, buds, and top of the foliage with an insecticide. Never spray rugosa roses because their foliage is easily damaged by chemical pesticides.

Spider mites

suck the sap from leaves and other tender parts of the rose which can lead to defoliation of the plant. The two-spotted spider mite is an insect often found in New England with the arrival of hot weather.

Symptoms: Spider mites cause the lowest foliage on the bush to turn yellow by sucking the juices from the leaves. If the leaves are examined on the underside, tiny salt-and-pepper spots can be seen. Tap the leaves over a white paper and the mites that fall off will look like small dots. They are tiny, but a magnifying glass will show you what they really look like, including the two spots on their backs. If the infestation is advanced, webbing is evident under the leaves. Look for spider mites in July when the weather turns hot.

Solutions: A light infestation can be controlled by a forceful spray of water on the undersides of the leaves which knocks spider mites to the ground where they will usually die. Since they reproduce every three days, spray with water every three days for a week or two. Lady beetles as well as lacewing larvae are beneficial insects that eat spider mites. Sometimes planting dill acts as a protection against spider mites. If the infestation is severe, a systemic miticide is effective when sprayed on the underside of the leaves. Spider mites can build up a resistance to miticides so it may be necessary to change miticides to effectively control this problem. Never spray rugosa roses because their foliage is easily damaged by chemical pesticides.

Japanese beetles

can be identified by their copper-colored bodies and green heads. In New England they can become a problem during July and early August. Japanese beetles feed on rose buds, blooms and leaves. White grubs, an early stage of development for Japanese beetles, are found under lawns in the grass roots. The grubs feed on the grass roots until winter, then burrow deeper into the soil to avoid freezing. When the weather turns warm again they feed on the grass roots until they mature and emerge as beetles in late June.

Symptoms: Dead areas in the lawn may indicate a colony of white grubs. The beetles are clearly evident on the plant during the day when they eat the foliage and blooms.

Solutions: Japanese beetles may be picked off the bush and dropped into water. Another control is to spray beetles with a spritz of *Windex* or ammonia mixed with seven parts of water. Some herbs such as thyme and parsley, as well as scented geraniums, are thought to act as protection against Japanese beetles. Avoid using Japanese beetle traps which will just attract more of them. To kill the larvae living in the lawn, treat the grass with a lawn care product that contains milky spore which is an effective long-term control. Effective chemical grub controls are readily available in garden centers, but the timing of the applications is important. Beetle larvae in the soil are vulnerable in late spring and again in late summer when they are close to the surface of the soil. Since there is no short-term solution to controlling grubs in the lawn, it may take several years to eliminate them. Neem oil may offer some limited control as will planting catnip, garlic and geraniums.

Leafrollers are small, green caterpillars that are found inside rolled leaves. Their eggs are deposited on the undersides of the leaves which are rolled into a protective cocoon-like covering.

Symptoms: Look for rolled leaves on plants. The rolled leaves, wrapped with webbing, serve as a cocoon for the eggs which develop into small green caterpillars which feed on the leaves.

Solutions: Remove the rolled leaves and destroy.

Diseases

As annoying as insects may be, they can be managed. Rose diseases, on the other hand, are the real menace to roses. The two most common diseases New England rose gardeners face are blackspot and powdery mildew, both fungal diseases.

Blackspot starts as small irregular black spots with fringed margins appearing on the upper sides of leaves with the surrounding leaf tissue turning yellow, creating sort of a halo effect. These spots get larger and may turn smudgy-looking with the entire leaf eventually turning yellow and dropping from the plant. Blackspot is spread by air currents and water splash, especially in warm, humid weather. It winters over on canes and fallen foliage which become the source of re-infection. Blackspot usually starts on the lower part of the plant and works its way up. While there are rose varieties that have demonstrated a remarkable resistance to blackspot, there are no roses that are completely immune to it. For novice rose gardeners, there are few garden events more discouraging than the seemingly mysterious arrival of blackspot. We remove any infected foliage we find both on the ground and on the plant, limiting the chances of re-infection. Our long range solution is replacing varieties that are vulnerable to diseases with more resistant roses. We are well underway with good results.

Powdery mildew appears as whitish-gray material forming on rosebuds and leaf tops. There are different species of this common fungal disease and each one has a small range of hosts. The species of powdery mildew that attacks lilac, for instance, has no effect on roses and vice versa. We have seen powdery mildew pop up in other gardens as early as mid-June, but it shows up later in the summer in our garden when warm days followed by cool nights in August provide ideal conditions. Our controls for powdery mildew are the same as for blackspot with the use of fungicides along with good garden hygiene.

As if this weren't enough to worry about, there are rose canker and botrytis, two more fungal diseases common in New England gardens. Canker appears in the early spring and starts with a pruning cut or wound of some kind which can be colonized by canker-causing fungi. The stems may turn yellow or show red spots that turn brown or black. The good news is that this occurs during cold spring weather and is far less likely to happen when temperatures rise and roses are actively growing. We prune off dead canes and stubs that may harbor this disease, plus our spray program for fungal diseases reduces canker problems. Ultimately, the best defense against canker is growing healthy roses.

Botrytis spores are spread by wind and rain and develop into a gray-black fuzzy mold on buds or blooms, particularly during cool, wet weather lasting over several days. It can develop anytime during the growing season when these conditions are favorable. Botrytis often happens on "balled" blooms, flowers that have started to open but stalled due to a lack of heat and sunlight. For us, botrytis is a minor problem occurring in the fall as our garden is slipping into dormancy. Our solution is very simple: prune off the plant parts affected, being careful to limit the release of dust-like spores to nearby plants, and discard.

There are also bacterial infections like crown gall, a spongy, tumor-like growth often found attached to the trunk near the bud union a few inches underground. Crown gall is contagious and the usual advice is to remove the entire plant from the garden and dispose of it. But on several occasions, we have removed galls from valuable rose varieties we wished to keep. We removed the soil in the immediate area of the gall and discarded it, then cut out the gall with a sharp knife, being sure to get all of it. Next, we treated the wound with an antibacterial product like *Bacitracin* and re-covered the affected area with fresh soil. We sanitized the larger tools by dipping them in a 5 percent bleach solution and swabbed smaller hand tools, like pruners, with isopropyl alcohol.

Although the appearance of rose diseases and insects may be discouraging, there are choices available to help control them. The remedies that you choose, as you will see, are personal decisions based on your level of tolerance for the damage caused by these garden pests.

Diseases: Symptoms, Causes & Solutions

Although the most common rose diseases in New England are blackspot and powdery mildew, other diseases may present themselves in your garden. Knowing what causes a disease and being on the lookout for known symptoms will help identify the problem so you can decide what remedies to use in order to keep a disease under control.

Blackspot is the most well-known fungal disease of outdoor roses. This fungus has been widely distributed with cultivated roses and no completely disease immune varieties are believed to exist. However, some current varieties are disease resistant and more new varieties are being introduced annually.

Symptoms: Black, sooty spots are visible on leaves. The spots tend to be round, varying in size from pinpoint to quarter-sized. Yellowing appears around the black spots and eventually the entire leaf turns yellow. Blackspot is first seen on the lower foliage of the plant. As the leaves yellow, they will start to drop. If the fungus is left untreated, it works its way through the entire rose bush. The infestation of blackspot can lead to a complete defoliation of the plant.

Causes: Blackspot thrives in moist conditions. Warm, humid, rainy weather provides ideal conditions for blackspot as does overhead watering. The fungus can over-winter in infected leaves, canes, and garden litter and moves via wind currents or splashing water.

Solutions: Remove infected leaves and debris from rose beds and discard them. Do not use infected leaves in compost. Using mulch helps prevent spores from splashing onto the bushes when they are watered. When watering, try to avoid wetting the leaves and water early in the day so any wet foliage will dry quickly. Prune and plant bushes far enough apart to provide good air circulation around and within bushes. Spraying with a fungicide is another alternative. The best solution, however, is to plant sustainable varieties with a known resistance to blackspot. Never spray rugosa roses because their foliage is easily damaged by chemical pesticides.

Powdery Mildew is another prevalent and serious fungal disease.

Symptoms: White or gray powdery growth appears on the leaf tops or undersides. Powdery mildew may also develop on new stems and forming buds, preventing the buds from opening properly. Leaves are curled, distorted or folded at mid-rib. This fungus can destroy young canes, stunt new growth and grow on sepals, peduncles and petals. Older leaves and stems may show no symptoms.

Causes: Powdery mildew typically occurs with warm days, high humidity, and cool nights. Spores are spread from plant to plant by wind. The spores can over-winter in infected leaves or stems.

Solutions: Good air circulation and ample sunlight in the garden is helpful in preventing powdery mildew. Prune away and remove infected plant material as the first level of defense. The use of a fungicide is an effective control. Never spray rugosa roses because their foliage is easily damaged.

Anthracnose is a disease sometimes confused with blackspot. It is a fungal disease often associated with climbers and ramblers although all roses are susceptible.

Symptoms: This disease starts out as small, round black spots which turn purple and brown, then light brown or tan. Eventually the centers of the spots turn white and are surrounded by a red or purple border. Small shot-holes may appear when the center of the spots drop away or crack. The leaves can turn yellow and defoliation can occur. The spots that result from anthracnose are usually more defined than those seen in blackspot.

Causes: The spores can over-winter on old leaves and canes. Anthracnose thrives in cool, moist spring conditions. It spreads via water or rain like blackspot.

Solutions: Remove old leaves from around the base of plants and prune out canes that are infected. Avoid overhead watering. The same spray program that is used for blackspot works for anthracnose. Never spray rugosa roses because their foliage is easily damaged.

Botrytis is another common fungus that affects roses as well as other plants.

Symptoms: Brown spots on petals or red-pink spots on lighter colored buds can be seen. Brown or gray fuzzy mold around blooms may appear.

Causes: Spores are transported by air or rain and can enter a plant through a wound or pruning cut. Botrytis occurs when there is high humidity and during rainy, cool periods. It is often seen in the fall.

Solutions: Removing and discarding infected parts of the plant are the simplest and best remedies. Maintaining good air circulation within and around the plants also helps.

Crown Gall is a serious bacterial infection of roses.

Symptoms: A spongy, round to irregular tumor type of tissue is commonly found growing at or below the bud union, or crown of the plant, often below soil level.

Causes: A soil-borne bacteria infects plants through wound sites on the roots or crown. The bacteria may live in the soil for many years.

Solutions: Inspect new plants before planting them. However, some plants may have latent infections which can become evident several years after planting. The plant may survive for years with a gall but could serve as a host for the bacteria. The best remedy is to remove the plant. In some cases soil removal is necessary to eliminate the bacteria. In other cases new roses have been successfully planted at the same site. Galls may be cut out of plants and the wounds treated with bleach or antibiotic creams. Sterilize pruners and other hand tools with isopropyl alcohol (not a bleach solution which may cause tools to rust) before and after treating galls. Sterilize large tools, like shovels, by dipping them into a bleach solution because a little rust on a shovel blade does no harm.

Downy Mildew is a fungal disease that occurs under moist conditions. All species of cultivated and wild roses are susceptible.

Symptoms: Leaves, stems and flowers may have purple to red or brown irregular blotches. Advanced infections will have yellowing of leaves with brown necrotic areas. There may be noticeable defoliation sometimes mistaken for spray damage. Downy mildew can defoliate an entire bush.

Causes: This systemic fungal disease is present in the soil and will begin to cause problems when night temperatures reach 55° to 65°F with 85 percent humidity.

Solutions: Cut back the defoliated plant and dispose of debris. Plant roses far enough apart for good air circulation. Avoid getting foliage wet. The use of a fungicide is an effective control. Never spray rugosa roses because their foliage is easily damaged.

Rose Canker is a fungus that affects older established roses as well as new roses. This fungus is most active when roses are not in a growth cycle, such as during the winter when they are dormant.

Symptoms: In the spring the stems turn yellow and sometimes have red spots. Then they turn brown or black.

Causes: Pruning cuts or wounds made in early spring become the entry point for germinating canker spores. During the months when roses are dormant, the fungus spreads.

Solutions: All infected and dead canes should be removed. When pruning, prune at an angle close to an active bud and be careful not to leave stubs. The use of a fungicide is an effective control. Never spray rugosa roses because their foliage is easily damaged.

Rose Mosaic Virus is transmitted by propagation and requires tissue-to-tissue contact. It cannot be spread by any other means.

Symptoms: The foliage may display a variety of yellow stripes or lines in a mosaic pattern or may not display any symptoms at all. Infected plants are slower to develop than healthy plants, produce fewer blooms of less quality, and have shorter life spans. Typical foliage symptoms can appear in the spring, disappear for a few weeks, and may reappear again. The symptoms may even disappear for a season or two, only to reappear again.

Causes: Infection spreads through tissue-to-tissue contact usually initiated by bud grafting at the propagation stage. If the bud or the root stock is infected with the virus, the resulting plant will also be infected.

Solutions: There is no cure for mosaic virus. Purchase only quality plants that have no symptoms of the disease. If you have an infected plant it will not spread to other plants in the garden and you may continue to grow that plant until it dies.

Rust is a fungus most often found on the west coast. Occasionally, roses infected with rust are found in New England due to the fact that they were shipped from the west coast with the disease. It cannot survive through a typical New England winter.

Symptoms: Spores that are light orange to yellow can be first noticed on the underside of leaves and then will appear on the upper sides. If plants have a lot of foliage the discoloration will be seen first on the bottom and in the middle of the plants.

Causes: Rust occurs where cool temperatures and high moisture are present during the prime growing season. Spores are transported by wind and can overwinter on leaves or infected canes.

Solutions: Remove infected canes and thin out densely growing bushes. This will reduce the level of moisture trapped in the center of the plant. The use of a fungicide is an effective control. Never spray rugosa roses because their foliage is easily damaged.

The Chutes' Garden

Planting, Pruning & Protecting Roses

New England gardeners who are new to roses often underestimate the importance of planting roses properly and overestimate the difficulty of pruning. They don't realize the value of winter protection until they discover dead or damaged bushes in the spring. Planting roses successfully is more than just digging a hole and placing a rose bush into it, and pruning roses is not a mysterious ritual. Winterizing roses is a simple practice that not only protects roses from winter's wrath, but also builds soil, too. This section focuses on the best ways to plant and prune roses as well as methods of protecting them from New England winters.

Winter Garden

Winter Protection—hilling up

CHAPTER 9

Planting

Spending some extra time thinking about how and where to plant your roses will yield dividends later on. While planting roses is pretty straightforward, there are a few guidelines that will get you off on the right foot and insure healthy, vigorous plants. Keep in mind what roses need: adequate sunlight, room to grow and good soil.

Before planting, select a location that receives at least six hours of direct, continuous sunlight daily. Roses are deciduous flowering shrubs and both the quantity and quality of the blooms hinge directly on the amount of sunlight they receive each day. If sunlight is in short supply, select those varieties that have the ability to bloom with less sunlight. *(See Chapter 5 for more details on the importance of sunlight.)* If trees shade your location of choice, then either thin their canopies, find another location, or, as a last resort, remove a tree or two.

When we moved into our current home in 1973, the property had a number of charming little maple trees that the previous owner had planted. Our newly planted gardens and the trees coexisted for a time, but the trees gradually grew into a small forest and hogged all the sunlight. One year we had an arborist come in and trim branches which allowed more sunlight to filter through, but this was only a temporary fix. After a season, the tree canopy came back fuller and lusher than ever, much to the detriment of our rose bushes. Tree roots, though, presented just as big a problem by invading the flower beds and stealing water and nutrients. One by one as the trees got old and sickly or grew too large for the property, we had them removed, leaving only one. This culling was done over a decade and the change of microclimate, though gradual, served to prevent any further decline of our rose gardens.

But in our front garden, when the underground pipes were continually clogged with tree roots, the two offending trees were removed in one shot. This sudden introduction of eight more hours of daily sunshine completely changed the plant dynamics and created a dramatic new microclimate. We took advantage of this now ideal location and planned a new sustainable rose garden. We replaced foundation plantings of yews, arborvitaes and junipers and the new rose garden sparkled from the very first day.

In addition to sunlight, another factor to consider is whether the planting area can accommodate the growth habit and size of the rose bush when it is fully grown. The first instinct is to plant roses too close together, but resist the urge to do this even though spacing them further apart will strike you as wasting space. Remember that the small rose in a two-gallon pot you plant in April may be three feet high and three feet wide by the middle of August and even larger the following year. In our new rose garden located in a very sunny area we were amazed at the difference in size of the same varieties growing in our shady back garden.

Generally speaking, allow at least 2½ to 3 feet between hybrid teas, grandifloras, and floribundas; 1 to 1½ feet between miniature roses. Give larger roses, such as many shrubs, old garden roses and climbers, more room. Plant roses even further apart if you are planning a sustainable garden where no pesticides will be applied. This extra space between plants allows for the circulation of air which helps prevent fungal diseases. Plan ahead when planting climbing roses and allow extra space for trellises, arbors, or fences.

Before planting a new garden, it's always a good idea to sketch out the size of the garden and location of each plant. Planning a garden on paper first prevents planting too many roses in too small a space. When designing our sustainable rose garden, we first measured the available planting area and decided we had to extend the beds by an additional foot. We needed 3 feet between the house and the bushes to have enough room to maintain the siding and also avoid the drip line of the wooden awnings over our windows. From past experience we knew that nothing could be planted under the front edge of the awnings because this is where rainwater cascades down the awnings onto the plants causing damage and potential backsplash.

Once we determined where the roses should be planted along the front of the house and the amount of space we had to work with, we made a scale drawing of our garden plan. We had already compiled a list of sustainable roses and noted their growth habits and colors. On our scale drawing we penciled in the varieties with large growth habits, placing them in the back of the garden, then added the designated spots for the other roses, using circles to indicate the placement of the planting holes. We reworked our plan, moving varieties around on paper until we were satisfied with color placement. Color determined our selection of varieties to a certain degree. Our decision to go with a "rainbow" garden meant planting different colors next to each other, thus avoiding two pink roses or two yellow roses side by side. Ordinarily, we like to design gardens with group plantings of the same variety for a mass effect. But in this garden with limited space, our multi-color rainbow objective did not allow for multiples of the same plant, so we planted one each of many varieties.

At the corner of our house we wanted a large rose to anchor and define the space and debated whether to plant a climbing rose which would require a trellis or support. Instead of a climber we decided on a large shrub rose that would make a statement and provide a visual impact, making the garden a defined space. To add a vertical dimension to the right of our front door in the arm of the L-shape of our house we chose a small climbing rose. On our drawing we left extra space between the rose and the house for a trellis. We amended our drawing several times before planting began, making certain that the placement between each rose gave us enough room to add daylilies, herbs, perennials, and spring bulbs as well as provide plenty of air circulation between each rose.

The final consideration before actual planting begins is evaluating the soil. Since no one is ever lucky enough to inherit perfect garden soil, it must be made. After we had all the foundation plants removed from the site where we would plant our sustainable rose garden, we were left with soil that had not been amended, fertilized, or improved in any way for fifty years—not ideal conditions in which to build a rose garden. Since building raised beds in the front garden was not part of our landscape design, we had an opportunity to see how quickly we could convert poor acidic soil into organic black gold.

The first thing we did was till the soil to check the soil composition and clean out any remaining roots. We not only found roots everywhere, but broken bottles, nails and other odd chunks of metal and construction debris from when the house was built in 1956. We felt like archeologists. The results showed a uniform foot or so of dusty top soil on top of processed sand. Not model conditions, but a soil situation that could be fixed with organic amendments.

We first applied lime followed by three inches of compost. We turned this in completely and then did it again. We let the beds lie fallow from spring, applying lime once again in the interim, until late fall when we planted the first rose bushes. Since then, we have added organic amendments throughout the beds each season in the form of horse manure and sometimes seaweed, used as winter protection. These locally available organics are then turned into the soil the following spring, adding to the deepening layer of crumbly, black top soil, perfect for roses and other flowers.

Another way to provide good soil for roses is to start from scratch and build your own in raised beds. Raised beds, 8 to 12 inches high, elevate plants from their surroundings and provide superior drainage. They are attractive, compensate for problems of poor soil and wrong pH, heat up faster in the spring, and are easier to work in. *(See more on raised beds in Chapter 4)*

Planting Bareroot Roses

Bareroot roses are dormant plants without soil on their roots. They can be planted anytime the ground is not frozen, but the best time to plant bareroot roses is in the early spring or late fall. We order catalog roses to arrive around April first; any sooner and we run the risk of the ground still being frozen. While April weather in New England can be capricious—cold and dreary one day, warm and balmy the next—the soil has typically thawed by then and bareroot roses can be planted. When we plant bareroot roses in the fall, we schedule them to arrive in mid-October and plant them right away.

Planting roses is a lot like baking a cake. Before we start planting, we gather our tools—shovel, wheelbarrow and trowel, plus all ingredients—pails of lime, superphosphate (or bone meal), water, organic material and, of course, the roses. Here's our "recipe."

1. Be prepared to plant bareroot roses soon after they arrive. They will be dehydrated to some degree so unpack them right away and submerge the roots completely in buckets of water. Then let them stand in a cool, shady place for twenty-four hours to rehydrate. They can remain in these buckets of water for a couple of days or up to a week in the extreme, but if you are unable to plant them within a week, then "heel" them in. Heeling in simply means laying the plants down in a shallow trench at a forty-five degree angle and covering the roots and most of the canes temporarily with an organic material like wood chips, soil, compost, seaweed, or horse manure and then watering well. This keeps your new roses moist and safe until you are ready to plant them. When planting day comes, carefully uncover the roses and place them back into the water buckets and leave them there until just before they are planted, always keeping their roots wet.

Bareroot Rose

2. Dig an oversized hole that will accommodate the roots. A hole 2 feet wide by 18 inches deep is usually big enough for a hybrid tea, but the size of the hole really depends on the size of the plant and the root mass. If in doubt, dig deeper and wider to insure the plant a long-range fertile environment.

3. Prune away any broken roots and trim extra long roots just enough to fit into the hole without bending. Remove any broken, weak, or twiggy canes as well as canes crossing the center of the plant. Be careful not to leave any stubs at the bud union or crown—the core of the plant where the roots meet the canes.

4. Place half the soil removed from the hole into a wheelbarrow and mix with an equal amount of organic material such as compost, composted horse manure, or leaf mold. If none of these are available, buy bags of composted products designed for this purpose. This enriched, amended soil now becomes your backfill.

5. Take one cup of lime and one cup of superphosphate (0-22-0) or bone meal and place half of each into the bottom of the planting hole. Mix the rest into the backfill in the wheelbarrow. The lime will raise the pH of our naturally acidic New England soil. Phosphate moves through soil so slowly that it is best to add it to the soil at the time of planting. (A soil test will determine pH and any deficiencies in your soil.)

Amended planting hole

6. Place the rose in the hole, spreading out its roots in their natural configuration without crowding or jamming them inside the hole. Make sure the bud union is two inches below the finished soil level in southern New England, deeper in the colder northern areas.

Planting with bud union below soil

7. Partially fill in the hole with the backfill and add water. Let drain.

8. Add more backfill, water in again and drain. DO NOT tamp the soil down with foot or shovel.

9. Finish backfilling the hole with the amended soil and water again. By mudding in the rose, air pockets are eliminated naturally and the plant is left in a moist environment in which to re-establish itself.

Mudding in

10. Hill or mound up the canes 12 inches or more with soil. If planted in the fall, this extra soil or mulch will serve as winter protection and can be left in place until spring. If planted in the spring, it prevents moisture loss through the canes on windy days. As the weather warms and the rose has established itself and shows signs of new growth, push the mound away, spreading the soil into the bed, and water frequently.

Planted rose with reservoir

11. Build a well with soil a few inches high around the base of the rose as a reservoir to hold water.

12. Water newly planted roses daily until they show signs of new growth.

13. Attach a plastic label with the name of the rose around a sturdy cane. The metal labels that come attached to the rose can fall off and get lost.

Planting Container-Grown Roses

Container-grown roses are bareroot roses that have been potted up prior to sale. We shop for local roses around the first of May, definitely before Mother's Day, when choices and supplies of the best varieties are the greatest. We look for superior, Number 1 graded roses with fresh, green, unwrinkled, and unblemished canes, plus lots of new growth, especially from the core of the plant. Unlike bareroot roses which have to be planted promptly, container-grown roses give you the option of planting at your convenience.

1. Water the container rose prior to planting and let drain. This hydrates the plant and makes it easier for the root ball to remain intact.

2. Dig a hole twice as wide as and a little deeper than the container.

3. Prepare the hole and soil, following steps 4 & 5 above.

4. Remove the rose from the container. If the rose is root bound, don't be afraid to pull apart some of the root mass with your fingers, enabling the roots to grow outward once planted. If the plant cannot be lifted out of the container easily, without the root ball falling apart, cut out the bottom of the container with a utility knife. Then, make a vertical cut down the side of the container and, holding the sides of the container firmly with both hands, place the container into the hole. Remove the rest of the container from around the rose and out of the hole.

5. Follow planting steps 6-13 above.

Miniature Roses

Miniature roses are started as rooted cuttings and may be quite small and tender when you receive them. We take whatever size pot they came in and re-pot them into the next larger size. We feed them regularly and provide plenty of water for a month or more so they can gain size as well as acclimate themselves to the conditions in our garden. At that point they can be planted. Often the minis look so good in the pot that we keep repotting them and use them for display anywhere we want them.

Transplanting Roses

Sometimes roses need to be moved. The rose bush may be too small, or more likely too large, for the spot where it is planted. Or maybe the rose was a disappointment in some way, and rather than throwing out an otherwise healthy plant, it can be passed along to a friend. Because tastes change and rose gardens are always works in progress, moving and removing roses are common practices. Our garden has only so many planting holes, so in order to add a new rose an existing rose bush has to go. There is an old wives' tale that says a rose should not be planted in the same hole where a rose has been removed. There is no horticultural basis to support this. We have used the same rose holes over and over again for years with excellent results. After removing a rose bush, we dig around in the hole, getting rid of roots and any pieces of the old rose. The soil in and around the old hole will get enriched with organic material when we replant.

Roses can be transplanted when dormant—in most of New England that means from mid-November through mid-March. We perform this annual ritual around Thanksgiving when we are certain that the garden has dropped into dormancy and before the ground freezes. Here's how we do it.

1. Prune the bush back by half, tie the canes together, if necessary, and water well the day before you plan to transplant.

2. Pre-dig and amend the soil for the new hole before digging up the bush to be transplanted. (*See steps 4 & 5 under Planting Bareroot Roses*)

3. Loosen the soil in a circle 12 inches out from the center of the plant with a shovel, creating a root ball—a larger plant will require a larger root ball. When the soil is loosened, carefully insert the shovel under the root ball and lift it out of the ground with as much of the root ball in tact as possible. Move it to the new hole in a wheelbarrow or, if it is a large plant, slide it onto a tarp and drag it.

4. Follow steps 6-13 under Planting Bareroot Roses as directed above. Be sure to water in well.

5. Keep the rose well-watered for two weeks or longer.

With a little practice, you will eventually develop your own unique planting routine. Planting roses is our rite of spring and a great way to open the season.

CHAPTER 10

Pruning

Roses are forgiving plants and it's almost impossible to permanently damage them with careless pruning. But nothing seems to confuse gardeners more than the seemingly complex nature of pruning roses. No wonder, since there is no single way to properly prune all types of roses. Hybrid teas, for instance, are pruned much differently than once-blooming old garden roses. One thing is certain: a spectacular garden full of well-tended roses with a full flush of color starts with careful pruning in early spring.

Spring pruning builds strong, healthy, and attractive plants. It encourages new growth, especially from the center of the plant and prepares roses for a robust first bloom. It increases flower production, controls the shape and size of the bush, and removes damaged and infected canes. It becomes the first defense against insects and diseases. Pruning takes practice and is best learned through experience, but here are a few guidelines that make pruning easier to understand.

Spring Pruning

Late March and early April, before the oaks and maples that surround our garden leaf out, is a special time. Strangely enough, with the trees barren, this is the brightest time of the year in the garden. The uncertain weather shifts from blustery, wintery cold one day to spring-like warmth the next. The weather makes no difference; we enjoy being out in the garden for the first time since Thanksgiving, cleaning up and getting ready for spring pruning.

Before pruning, let's make a distinction between everblooming and once-blooming roses. Everblooming, or repeat blooming roses, like hybrid teas and floribundas, are plants that bloom and re-bloom several times each season on stems and canes produced in the current season. These new stems and canes are known as *new wood*. Once-bloomers, on the other hand, like many old garden roses and climbers, have only one, usually lengthy, bloom period and these blooms grow on stems and canes produced in previous seasons. These canes are referred to as *old wood*. As you will see later, this is an important distinction.

Early springtime is the only time roses are completely without foliage, exposing the bones or skeleton of each bush. This is the best time to examine all roses, both everblooming as well as once-blooming, and prune out the 3 D's: dead, diseased or damaged canes which are clearly visible. Decisions regarding crossing canes and overall shape, especially on large plants, are much easier to make now than they will be in a few weeks when newly emerging foliage may mask problems. Postpone further pruning on once-blooming roses until later in the season.

Before Spring Pruning

After Spring Pruning

White pith

Everblooming Roses

Continue additional pruning of everblooming roses *(See How to Prune below)* when the bright yellow forsythia flowers arrive, heralding the arrival of spring—that's mid-April for us in southern New England. Blooming forsythia indicates that both the soil and air temperatures are warm enough to initiate plant growth and beneficial microorganisms in the soil that process nutrients are no longer dormant.

The exact timing of spring pruning, though, is not critical. April is a fickle month in New England, with the potential for late season frosts and even snowstorms. Cold temperatures and foul weather can damage tender, newly emerging growth. It does no harm to wait an extra week or two after the forsythia blooms to finish pruning since roses will catch up by mid-June.

Once-blooming Roses

Once-blooming roses are a different story. After pruning out any dead, diseased and damaged canes in early spring, hold off on any other fine tuning until after they have finished blooming, usually by the Fourth of July. Additional pruning and deadheading at this time will stimulate new growth during the rest of the season. This subsequent new growth will be the canes on which next year's roses will bloom. Because these varieties bloom on year-old wood, it is easy to see that careless spring pruning of these varieties, beyond dead or diseased canes, could eliminate healthy canes and stems before they had a chance to flower.

Timing the Bloom Cycle

It's possible to strategically prune everblooming roses after the first or second bloom cycle goes by so the next bloom cycle coincides with a specific event later in the summer or even in the early autumn. Each variety has its own built-in timetable for re-bloom based on the number of petals in the bloom and other genetically determined factors. A heavily petaled hybrid tea will require fifty-five or more days to recycle from one bloom period to the next, while many floribundas will rebloom in forty days or less. We have found that fifty days is a reliable average that we know works for a garden of mixed, repeating roses in southern New England. Bear in mind that mid-summer weather is the wild card when a few days of rain or a heat wave can skew the schedule.

Simply count back fifty days from your target date and prune off every bud and bloom on each rose bush, then cross your fingers—timing nature is serendipitous work with no guarantees. Having said that, we have successfully timed roses to bloom for weddings and parties and we once timed the second bloom of thirty pots of miniature roses to serve as favors for a Midsummer Night's Dream event in August. If it works, we take the credit. If not, we blame Mother Nature.

Pruning Tools

You need only a few hand tools to prune roses. The primary tool is a pair of pruning shears that effectively cuts canes up to a half-inch in diameter. We like "by-pass" pruners which have two opposing curved blades that slide pass each other and cut like a scissors. There are plenty of choices in pruners, so try out as many models as you can and purchase the one that feels the most comfortable. Many reasonably priced models are available that will do the job as long as you keep them sharp. The more expensive models have replaceable stainless steel parts that can be disassembled for cleaning and sharpening and will last a lifetime. We also use small, inexpensive hand pruners with one-inch blades and blunted tips that slip nicely into a back pocket or even into a sport coat pocket. Investing in a sheath that attaches to a belt makes it easy to carry pruners in the garden where there is always some pruning and grooming necessary.

For pruning thicker canes, loppers are ideal. They have long handles made of wood or aluminum that provide leverage when cutting canes up to 1½ inches in diameter. Loppers come as by-pass models also.

Pruning saws are great for removing large, gnarly, old woody canes. There are many sizes to choose from, but the short models with a fine-toothed blade that fold up into the handle like a jackknife are a good choice. This type gets into tight places and makes short work of the heaviest canes. It also fits nicely into a garden tool bag.

A pair of hedge clippers is handy for shearing densely flowering varieties. They quickly trim away hundreds of small, spent blooms from landscape roses, re-setting them for their next bloom cycle.

Well-maintained tools make nice clean cuts—good for the roses as well as making the job of pruning easier. Keeping keen edges on pruning gear is easily done with a sharpening stone or file. A black residue from rose sap builds up on the sides of pruner blades during the season and can be rubbed off with fine sand paper. Squirting *WD-40* or a few drops of other lubricants on all moving parts from time to time keeps the moving parts working smoothly. To prevent the spread of disease we occasionally dip pruning blades into isopropyl alcohol which disinfects without rusting. Although some rust from normal wear and tear in the garden is inevitable, it can be removed with a few swipes of fine sandpaper and a wipe with an oiled cloth.

Finally, anyone working with roses quickly discovers thorns and the need for gloves. We have several pairs of gloves: a pair of thorn-proof leather gloves that protect hands, wrists, and arms; and a pair of rubberized gloves to use for wet work like planting and potting up in the spring.

How to Prune

Start by pushing any winter protection away from the center of the plant, then remove the dead, diseased, or damaged canes. Dead canes are easily recognized as brown or black canes. These should be pruned back to the bud union or crown of the plant, if necessary. Cut cleanly, leaving no stubs on which disease could grow later. Next, prune away any damaged or diseased wood such as broken or wounded canes—canes with dark lesions caused by canker, for instance—and prune below the damage. Dead, damaged or diseased canes can and should be pruned from any rose at any time of the season.

Even if all the canes have turned black, do not assume that the plant is dead. After a particularly cold winter a few years ago, one entire bed of hybrid teas in our garden had nothing but black canes poking out of the winter cover like some noir scene from a Stephen King novel. When pruning day came in April, the winter cover was pushed away from the center of the plants revealing healthy green canes. The portion of each cane that was above the manure mounds that we used as winter protection was black. The portion that was covered by the mounds was green and alive. Even when a rose bush seems to be absolutely dead in spring, wait a few more weeks until the weather is uniformly warm before removing it. Hardy own-root roses can die back to the roots and still come back when the soil temperatures warm up.

Next, inspect each cane for swollen active bud eyes, or growth buds, that indicate healthy tissue and cut a quarter inch above an outside facing growth bud. This stimulates new stems to grow away from the center of the plant. Look for the pith, or cross-section of the cut, to resemble a freshly cut apple. If there is any brown staining in the pith, remove a little more of the cane until you find that creamy white color.

Check for *suckers*. These are stems growing from the rootstock below the bud union on grafted plants. If left alone, they will eventually take over the entire rose bush, killing off the grafted part of the plant. Suckers can be identified because their foliage and blooms are distinctly different from the rest of the rose bush. They should be pruned off as close as possible to the trunk of the rootstock to prevent them from growing back.

All other pruning depends on the type and growth habit of the rose.

- **Hybrid teas and grandifloras**
  Cutting back any winter-damaged, dead or diseased canes on hybrid teas and grandifloras may be radical and it will take some courage for novice rose gardeners to keep cutting to find that creamy pith. (Be aware that after a very cold winter, hybrid teas and grandifloras may need to be pruned to within a few inches of the bud union.) If you are uncertain where to make your cuts, first prune conservatively in April, and then go back and re-prune two weeks later. The emerging new growth will make pruning decisions easier. Open up the center of the plant by cutting away any weak, twiggy growth and removing any crossing canes, allowing in light and air. Finally, shape your rose, leaving three to six canes.

- **Floribundas**
  Leave more wood on floribundas by cutting them back no more than one third, thinning out the center and shaping the plant to leave a nice natural form. Floribundas are flower factories and the goal here is to have a mass display of color—more stems and canes mean more blooms.

- **Shrub roses, old garden roses, and species roses**
  Prune in moderation. Once any dead, damaged, or diseased wood is removed, shape the bushes, leaving them full and natural looking. Remove no more than a quarter of the bush. On mature bushes, occasionally eliminate a few older, woody canes to stimulate new growth. The bark on these old canes is gray and looks old, making them easy to identify. Prune once-blooming roses as soon as the flowering is done.

- **Miniature Roses**
  These can be carefully pruned in the spring like hybrid teas or thinned boldly, removing half the stems with hedge clippers and fine-tuning with hand pruners. Four weeks later you won't be able to tell the difference.

- **Climbing roses**
  Other than the removal of dead, damaged or diseased wood, prune climbers sparingly in the spring. Postpone additional pruning until after the first bloom. Remember, many once-blooming climbing varieties bloom on old wood; allow them to bloom first before any pruning is done. Train growing canes horizontally on arbors, garden structures, and along fences. This horizontal nature enhances the development of lateral shoots—stems growing from the main canes—and these are the major flower producers on climbing roses. Keeping the laterals properly deadheaded will allow everblooming varieties to repeat all summer.

Finish by cleaning up and discarding all the pruned material as well as any accumulated winter debris. An optional step you can take is to cover the pruning cuts with white glue or other sealers available for this purpose. This acts as a defense against disease and insects, such as cane borers, from invading the plant.

Deadheading

Deadheading is the process of removing spent blooms to re-set roses for their next bloom cycle. It is a necessary practice to ensure the continuation of flower production on any everblooming variety. Without deadheading, roses may continue on to the production of seeds and not more flowers. Once-blooming varieties are deadheaded right after their bloom cycle finishes.

To deadhead, cut the stem of the spent bloom back to a quarter inch above a growth bud at a point thick enough to support a new stem and flower. Growth buds can be found at the leaf axil where the leaf meets the stem. Roses have compound leaves made up of leaflets growing along a common axis. A well-known rule of thumb is to prune at a five-leaflet leaf, where a growth bud is located, and the next stem will likely grow. While this is true, do not be too dogmatic about this because growth buds can be found at a seven or even a nine-leaflet leaf.

Any densely flowering varieties, such as landscape varieties planted en masse with an abundance of spent blooms, can be deadheaded successfully with hedge clippers. Shear the old blooms away, shaping the plant at the same time, and finish by fine-tuning with hand pruners. This avoids the tedium of hand pruning hundreds of old blooms from extremely floriferous varieties. This may seem severe, but the roses will rebloom nicely in forty to fifty days.

An alternative method of deadheading is to simply snap off the faded bloom by hand or with pruners. This stimulates new growth from several growth buds lower down the stem and is an ideal technique that adds size to first-year rose bushes.

Use good judgment when pruning during the growing season and keep as much foliage as possible on the plant because leaves produce food. If the rose bush is large enough, space deadheading over several days in order to keep more foliage on the plant.

Disbudding

Disbudding is the act of removing secondary rose buds in order to produce a large, single flower at the end of the stem. Removal of all buds as they emerge below the primary bloom forces the entire stem's energy into developing one superior flower. Finger prune by rubbing or pinching off emerging buds by hand or with small pruners as they develop.

Roses that bloom in sprays or clusters have a *terminal bud*, the bud that grows in the center of the spray. This bud is easy to identify. It develops sooner than the other buds and will open first. The other buds often will wait until it goes by. Pinch this terminal bud out as soon as it can be identified and the remaining buds in the spray will open together.

Pruning roses is not complicated. With common sense and a little practice every rose gardener will be able to improve both the quality and the quantity of their blooms as well as build strong, healthy, and vigorous rose bushes.

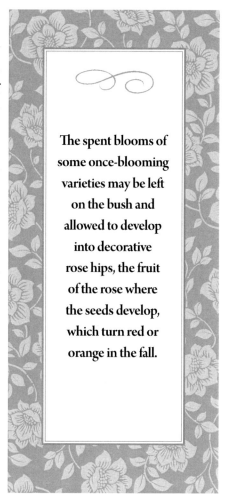

The spent blooms of some once-blooming varieties may be left on the bush and allowed to develop into decorative rose hips, the fruit of the rose where the seeds develop, which turn red or orange in the fall.

CHAPTER 11

Winter Protection

By any definition New England winters are cold. New England rose gardeners accept the challenge that winter weather presents and have developed successful winter survival strategies that preserve their rose bushes regardless of how low temperatures go. New England, in its compact corner of the northeast, ranges from Zone 3 and 4 in the northernmost parts of Maine, Vermont, and New Hampshire, where temperatures can plummet to -35° F in January, all the way to Zone 7 in southern Rhode Island where the thermometer rarely goes below zero. Central New England is primarily Zones 4 and 5 where the coldest temperatures can drop to -20° F or even -25° F, more than cold enough to kill or damage many varieties. Southern New England is mostly Zone 6 where the coldest temperatures can be as low as -10°F.

Winter survival begins with the selection of winter hardy varieties and proper planting. Many tough shrub, species, and old garden roses can tolerate the most bitter cold on their own while other zone-appropriate varieties will do just as well with some measure of help. This winter protection, applied after roses go dormant in the fall, allows New England gardeners to successfully grow many types of roses despite the coldest of winters. Adding winter protection saves plant size, too. Even hardy roses may suffer some winterkill on canes and stems that will have to be pruned away in the spring which diminishes the size of roses, especially climbers. This loss can be minimized, especially during an unusually cold winter, by providing adequate winter protection.

Besides choosing winter hardy varieties and planting them properly, the next line of defense against winter damage is insuring that roses are healthy going into the winter season. Accomplish this by following the basic steps of rose care—keeping roses watered, fertilized, and disease-free. Often roses die not directly from the cold but because they were weakened by disease and a lack of proper care prior to the winter weather, making them easy prey despite good winterizing measures.

To survive a New England winter once roses become dormant, they must stay dormant. Dormancy is that part of the life cycle of roses when growth, both above and below ground, is temporarily suspended. This is the plant's defense mechanism against bitter cold and windy weather. The onset of dormancy is determined by two major environmental cues: dropping temperatures and diminishing daylight. Believe it or not, this process begins in August as periods of daylight become noticeably shorter and nights become cooler.

When a rose slowly slips into dormancy over a period of several months, cell walls gradually thicken and water within the cells is transformed into an antifreeze of sorts. Varieties that are able to achieve this transition successfully are said to be winter hardy. Rose gardeners can assist this process in several ways. First, stop feeding roses sixty days prior to the first frost. Our final feeding is in early August. Next, stop deadheading in late summer and early fall. Deadheading is a form of pruning that stimulates end-of-season growth that will not have time to mature. When deadheading ceases, rose hips form and swell with seeds, thereby ending flower production for the season.

Once dormant, many roses require some degree of winter protection, not to keep them warm but to keep them dormant during mid-winter freeze/thaw cycles. Typical New England weather features extremes in mid-winter temperatures. One or two unusually warm January days can provide false signals to plants that it is time to break dormancy and start growing. Water begins to rise in rose canes and when temperatures inevitably drop back to seasonal levels, water in those canes freezes and expands, rupturing cells and causing permanent damage called winterkill. Keeping roses cold and dormant by applying winter protection in late fall can prevent much of this damage. Without winter protection, tender varieties become vulnerable to cold damage when the thermometer drops below 25° F. Most hybrid teas, grandifloras, and floribundas are not at risk until temperatures fall between 10 and 20° F. However, there are rugosas and very hardy shrub and old garden roses that can survive bitter cold temperatures down to -30° F without any protection.

The ideal time to apply winter protection is after the first hard frost. Since this varies year to year, even area to area, depending on the microclimate of your garden, target mid to late November. Winterizing too early keeps the soil around each rose bush artificially warm and actually serves to delay dormancy.

We usually winterize on Thanksgiving weekend. We start with very light pruning and secure long canes to prevent them from being whipped about during winter storms.

Heavy pruning is postponed until spring since it can retard dormancy by stimulating new growth at a time when rose bushes need to fall asleep. In addition, it's a good idea to leave some sacrificial wood on those varieties that could suffer some degree of winterkill that we know will be cut away in the spring.

Next, since diseases can winter over in fallen foliage, we rake up garden litter and debris and discard it. Then we apply lime, if necessary, to maintain proper pH; winter snow and rain will wash it in. We finish by using the hilling up method described below.

Methods of Winter Protection

- **Hilling up:** This method involves using soil, manure, seaweed, compost or mulch to hill up, or mound, the base of each rose to a height of 12 inches to shelter the vulnerable bud union. In the spring, this mound of organic material can be pulled away from the plant and spread into the rose bed thus enriching the soil. We prefer horse manure and utilize this simple, fast, and effective method and lose very few roses to winterkill regardless of how cold it gets.

- **Rose collars:** Another technique involves wrapping a collar of chicken wire, newspapers, or tar paper, twelve inches high, around each rose and backfilling it with compost, shredded oak leaves, mulch or manure. Collars prevent the backfill material from being blown around by winter winds.

- **Rose cones:** These are made of Styrofoam and look like inverted ice cream cones. Cut the bush back enough to fit inside the cone. Weigh the cone down to prevent it from becoming air borne in windy winter weather and drill a few holes to provide ventilation.

- **Thermal blankets:** Canadian rose gardeners prune their tender roses to twelve inches and cover the entire bed with a quarter-inch white thermal blanket laid over a wooden frame. Once snow covers the blanket, the temperature inside stays constant all winter regardless of the weather outside.

- **Snow:** Snow all by itself is an excellent insulator. It maintains a constantly cold temperature underneath and prevents drastic swings of temperatures from occurring too rapidly, insuring dormancy. Snow also acts as protection from winter winds that can desiccate rose canes.

Climbers

To safeguard climbing roses, we protect the bud union by hilling up the base of the plant and tie all long canes securely to their supports. This provides enough winter protection for gardens in Zones 5 and 6. Whatever winterkill we have only affects the tips of each cane and we snip that away in the spring.

In colder areas, long canes are wrapped in burlap or other breathable insulating material to protect them from drying out in desiccating wintery winds. Rose gardeners in northern New England and Canada detach their climbers from their supports, lay the long canes on the ground and cover them with thermal blankets, soil, or some other organic material. It's extra work but the only way these gardeners can maintain long canes of varieties that would otherwise be considerably shortened each year due to winterkill.

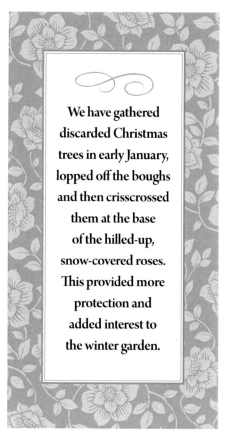

We have gathered discarded Christmas trees in early January, lopped off the boughs and then crisscrossed them at the base of the hilled-up, snow-covered roses. This provided more protection and added interest to the winter garden.

Roses in Containers

Roses in containers present a different challenge. If left exposed above ground all winter, the entire plant—especially the roots—is vulnerable to winter damage. Check to make sure roses are planted in plastic pots since clay and ceramic pots will crack when the soil inside freezes. Here are several strategies of protecting roses in containers.

- Here's how we do it. Because we have over 100 containers, we assemble "cribs" made from plywood cut into 2 feet x 4 feet segments. We first stack the containers tightly together in several rows against a fence and then surround them on the other three sides with enough plywood sheets, held in place with concrete blocks, creating a crib. Then we carefully shovel woodchips or shredded oak leaves over the top. In the spring, it's a simple matter of removing the sides, clearing out the organic insulating material, then stacking the plywood and blocks out of the way.

- If you only have a few containers, place them against a protected wall and cover with leaves or wood chips.

- Cover the containers. Gather them together and cover the top and all four sides completely with wood chips or whatever handy organic material is available.

- Bury the containers. Dig a trench, place the containers inside and cover them with woodchips or mulch. This is very effective, but a considerable amount of work.

- Bring the containers inside. Water well and place the roses in an unheated cellar or garage. Water occasionally all winter. This method is not ideal because the soil dries out, despite watering. Plus the plants tend to leave dormancy too early and results in white spindly growth due to lack of light.

Mid-winter in New England is a cold time for roses. The last two weeks of January are traditionally the coldest period of the year and some form of winter protection is necessary to safeguard those roses that require it. But if you have correctly planted zone-appropriate varieties and provided basic rose care throughout the growing season, your roses will have no problem surviving any New England winter.

Westerland & Baby Love

Sustainable Roses

Sustainable roses, winter hardy varieties that remain healthy and attractive without the use of pesticides, have been around for a very long time. Many shrub roses and old garden roses grow remarkably well in cemeteries and old homesteads on benign neglect, living without pesticides, subsisting on rainwater and whatever nutrients they can absorb from the surrounding soil. It's not that they are immune to attacks from insects and diseases; they aren't. But these tough plants have a genetic ability to endure these assaults, even losing their foliage annually from fungal diseases and yet survive bitter winter cold that would kill a lesser plant.

This toughness and inherent sustainability was compromised in large measure in the mid-nineteenth century with the arrival of hybrid teas—roses prized more for their flower form, color, and repeat bloom—than for their ability to resist cold weather and common rose diseases. Chemical pesticides became the solution to successfully manage garden pests in attractive but temperamental varieties. This use of chemicals, however, has rapidly lost favor in recent years for several reasons. Primarily, the gardening public, in general, considers chemical pesticides unacceptably toxic and desires other more environmentally friendly alternatives. Secondly, many effective pesticides have been removed from the retail market with only costly alternatives remaining. This leaves sustainability as the only sensible option.

Sustainability as a concept is not new. It became a major hybridizing objective for a legion of rose breeders. Early in the twentieth century, Rhode Island's Walter Brownell realized long before anyone else the long term benefit of what he called "Sub-Zero" roses—resilient roses that would flourish in the New England climate. Dr. Griffith Buck from Iowa State University knew that if roses were too difficult to grow, gardeners would find something else, and he spent an entire career developing winter hardy varieties. Dr. Felicitas Svejda, a plant geneticist and rose breeder for Agriculture Canada in the last half of the twentieth century, developed the Explorer Series of extremely hardy shrub roses bred to thrive in the harsh Canadian climate. Meilland International in France began introducing easy-to-grow varieties, free flowering roses on strong plants, in the mid-1960's. More recently, Ping Lim, whose major objective is sustainability, created the Easy Elegance series of attractive and durable roses when at Bailey Nurseries in Minnesota. Varieties from all of these pioneers as well as many other hybridizers are included in our sustainable rose list in the following chapter.

Our selection process is based on two factors: winter hardiness and resistance to common fungal diseases. A variety's level of winter hardiness is essential, since if it is not able to survive a New England winter, it won't matter how disease resistant it is. Therefore, we include only those varieties that are rated for Zone 6 and colder. Keep in mind that when deciding on varieties, there is some latitude between adjacent zones. For example, varieties hardy in Zone 6 may do quite well in Zone 5 if given winter protection; but be reasonable, if you live in Zone 4, don't choose a rose rated for Zone 6 because survival is unlikely regardless of the amount of winter protection you provide.

From these zone-appropriate roses, we chose varieties that have a demonstrated resistance to common fungal diseases. We based our choices on our own rose growing experiences for the past twenty years, as well as our observations of how varieties performed in public and private gardens where chemical pesticides are not used. We also researched the performance of varieties and received input from other experienced New England rosarians. Along with more recent introductions, we intentionally included a selection of older varieties, even one that dates back to 1581. These old favorites have long since withstood the test of time and became the early champions of sustainability. We then further narrowed our list down to those varieties that are commercially available. All varieties listed can be found locally or through mail order sources.

This list is certainly not inclusive. Other varieties could have been added, but our goal is to provide a collection of roses that offer New England gardeners a choice of growth habit, bloom size, degree of fragrance and color. Most of the roses in our list are everblooming. If a variety is once-blooming, it is noted in the comments section of our description. Also noted in the comments section is whether a rose is designated as an EarthKind™ rose, a rose that has displayed a high level of disease resistance after being field-tested under the direction of Texas AgriLife Extension Service, a part of Texas A&M. Many of the roses we chose are shrub roses, but there are also species roses, polyanthas, floribundas, large-flowered climbers and a selection of old garden roses.

Since the level of disease resistance depends on environmental conditions, the microclimates in which they are grown, and the kind of care they receive, the level of sustainability will vary from garden to garden. What all these varieties do share, however, is the ability to survive New England winters and remain relatively healthy and attractive without the use of chemical pesticides.

CHAPTER 12

Sustainable Roses for New England

A̶n Abbreviation Key will be found at the end of this list. Heights listed are approximate and will vary from zone to zone. Blooms are listed as Single (5-12 petals), Semi-double (13-25 petals), Double (26-40 petals), and Very Double (over 40 petals). Varieties with an asterisk can be found in our Photo Gallery.

Alain Blanchard

Class:	Gallica (OGR)	Year:	1839
Hybridizer	Vibert	Color:	Mauve
Blooms:	Semi-double	Hardiness:	Zone 5
Fragrance:	Moderate	Height:	4´- 5´
Comments:	Spotted blooms; bright gold stamens; thorny		

Alexander MacKenzie

Class:	Shrub	Year:	1985
Hybridizer:	Svejda	Color:	Red blend
Blooms:	Very double	Hardiness:	Zone 3/4
Fragrance:	None	Height:	6´
Comments:	Agr. Canada Explorer Series; excellent disease resistance		

Alika

Class:	Gallica (OGR)	Year:	1906
Hybridizer:	Hansen	Color:	Medium Red
Blooms:	Single to semi-double	Hardiness:	Zone 3
Fragrance:	Moderate	Height:	6´
Comments:	Shade tolerant; yellow stamens; once-blooming		

All the Rage *

Class:	Shrub	Year:	2008
Hybridizer:	Lim	Color:	Apricot blend
Blooms:	Semi-double	Hardiness:	Zone 4
Fragrance:	None	Height:	3´
Comments:	Easy Elegance rose; apricot bloom, yellow center; own-root		

Allamand-Ho

Class:	Shrub	Year:	1984
Hybridizer:	Buck	Color:	Pink blend
Blooms:	Double	Hardiness:	Zone 5
Fragrance:	Moderate	Height:	4´
Comments:	Yellow pink flowers with sweet fragrance		

Aloha

Class:	Cl HT	Year:	1949
Hybridizer:	Boerner	Color:	Medium Pink
Blooms:	Very Double	Hardiness:	Zone 5
Fragrance:	Strong	Height:	8´
Comments:	Can be grown as shrub or climber; apple fragrance		

Altissimo

Class:	LCl	Year:	1966
Hybrizier:	Delbard-Chabert	Color:	Medium Red
Blooms:	Single	Hardiness:	Zone 5
Fragrance:	Slight	Height:	10´
Comments:	Large single blooms		

America

Class:	LCl	Year:	1976
Hybridizer:	Warriner	Color:	Orange-pink
Blooms:	Very Double	Hardiness:	Zone 5/6
Fragrance:	Strong	Height:	10´ - 12´
Comments:	AARS 1976; coral pink blooms; spicy fragrance		

American Pillar

Class:	HWich (rambler)	Year:	1902
Hybridizer:	Van Fleet	Color:	Pink blend
Blooms:	Single	Hardiness:	Zone 5
Fragrance:	None	Height:	12´ - 20´
Comments:	Dark pink flowers with white eye and golden stamens; grows in clusters; once-blooming		

Apothecary's Rose

Class:	Species (Gallica)	Year:	Before 1600
Hybridizer:	Wild Rose	Color:	Deep Pink
Blooms:	Semi-double	Hardiness:	Zone 3/4
Fragrance:	Slight	Height:	3'- 4'
Comments:	aka *R. gallica officinalis*; shade tolerant; once-blooming; dark pink blooms with golden yellow stamens		

Applejack

Class:	Shrub	Year:	1973
Hybridizer:	Buck	Color:	Pink blend
Blooms:	Semi-double	Hardiness:	Zone 3/4
Fragrance:	Moderate	Height:	6'
Comments:	Apple fragrance; can be grown as climber or bush		

Baby Love

Class:	Miniature	Year:	1992
Hybridizer:	Scrivens	Color:	Deep Yellow
Blooms:	Single	Hardiness:	Zone 4/5
Fragrance:	Slight	Height:	3'
Comments:	Small single cheery blooms; flowers all season		

Ballerina *

Class:	HMsk (shrub)	Year:	1937
Hybridizer:	Bentall	Color:	Medium Pink
Blooms:	Single	Hardiness:	Zone 4/5
Fragrance:	None	Height:	6'
Comments:	Small pink flowers with white eye grow in large clusters; constant blooms		

Belinda's Dream

Class:	Shrub	Year:	1992
Hybridizer:	Basye	Color:	Medium Pink
Blooms:	Very Double	Hardiness:	Zone 5
Fragrance:	Moderate	Height:	4'
Comments:	Earth Kind Rose; good in heat, humidity		

Belle de Crecy

Class:	Gallica (OGR)	Year:	1829
Hybridizer:	Hardy	Color:	Mauve
Blooms:	Very double	Hardiness:	Zone 4/5
Fragrance:	Strong	Height:	6'
Comments:	Fragrant, very double blooms; almost thornless		

Belle Poitevine

Class:	HRg (shrub)	Year:	1894
Hybridizer:	Bruant	Color:	Medium Pink
Blooms:	Semi-double	Hardiness:	Zone 3/4
Fragrance:	Strong	Height:	3´
Comments:	Orange hips; very hardy		

Blanc Double de Coubert

Class:	HRg (shrub)	Year:	1892
Hybridizer:	Cochet-Cochet	Color:	White
Blooms:	Semi-double	Hardiness:	Zone 3/4
Fragrance:	Strong	Height:	5´
Comments:	Wrinkled rugosa foliage; tolerates shade		

Blushing Knock Out *

Class:	Shrub	Year:	2004
Hybridizer:	Yoder	Color:	Light Pink
Blooms:	Single	Hardiness:	Zone 4/5
Fragrance:	Slight	Height:	4´
Comments:	Low maintenance; shade tolerant; sport of Knock Out		

Bonanza

Class:	Shrub	Year:	1982
Hybridizer:	Kordes	Color:	Yellow blend
Blooms:	Semi-double	Hardiness:	Zone 6
Fragrance:	Slight	Height:	4´-5´
Comments:	Glossy foliage; blooms in clusters		

Bonica

Class:	Shrub	Year:	1985
Hybridizer:	Meilland	Color:	Medium Pink
Blooms:	Double	Hardiness:	Zone 4
Fragrance:	Slight	Height:	4´
Comments:	First shrub to win World's Favorite Rose 2003; AARS 1987		

Brite Eyes

Class:	LCl	Year:	2006
Hybridizer:	Radler	Color:	Pink blend
Blooms:	Single	Hardiness:	Zone 5
Fragrance:	Moderate	Height:	6´-8´
Comments:	Light, spicy fragrance		

Buffalo Gal

Class:	HRg (shrub)	Year:	1989
Hybridizer:	Edland	Color:	Deep Pink
Blooms:	Semi-double	Hardiness:	Zone 3
Fragrance:	Strong	Height:	4´
Comments:	aka Foxi Pavement; spicy fragrance; red hips		

Caldwell Pink

Class:	Polyantha	Year:	1928
Hybridizer:	Lilley	Color:	Medium Pink
Blooms:	Semi-double	Hardiness:	Zone 5/6
Fragrance:	None	Height:	4´
Comments:	aka Pink Pet; Earth Kind Rose		

Camaieux

Class:	Gallica (OGR)	Year:	1830
Hybridizer:	Gendron	Color:	Mauve striped
Blooms:	Very Double	Hardiness:	Zone 4/5
Fragrance:	Strong	Height:	4´
Comments:	Striped rose; shade tolerant		

Cape Diamond

Class:	HKor (shrub)	Year:	2007
Hybridizer:	Bedard	Color:	Medium Pink
Blooms:	Double	Hardiness:	Zone 3/4
Fragrance:	Moderate	Height:	4´
Comments:	Spicy fragrance; moss buds		

Captain Samuel Holland

Class:	Shrub	Year:	1991
Hybridizer:	Ogilvie	Color:	Medium Red
Blooms:	Semi-double	Hardiness:	Zone 3/4
Fragrance:	Slight	Height:	6´
Comments:	Agr. Canada Explorer Series; grown as shrub or climber		

Carefree Beauty *

Class:	Shrub	Year:	1977
Hybridizer:	Buck	Color:	Medium Pink
Blooms:	Semi-double	Hardiness:	Zone 4/5
Fragrance:	Slight	Height:	5´
Comments:	Earth Kind Rose; large blooms; orange-red hips		

Carefree Celebration

Class:	Shrub	Year:	2007
Hybridizer:	Radler	Color:	Apricot blend
Blooms:	Semi-double	Hardiness:	Zone 5
Fragrance:	None	Height:	5′
Comments:	Landscape rose		

Carefree Delight *

Class:	Shrub	Year:	1994
Hybridizer:	Meilland	Color:	Pink blend
Blooms:	Single	Hardiness:	Zone 4
Fragrance:	None	Height:	4′
Comments:	AARS 1996; white eye; orange hips; landscape rose		

Carefree Marvel

Class:	Shrub	Year:	2003
Hybridizer:	Meilland	Color:	Deep Pink
Blooms:	Double-Very Double	Hardiness:	Zone 5
Fragrance:	Moderate	Height:	2′- 3′
Comments:	Shade tolerant; landscape rose		

Carefree Spirit

Class:	Shrub	Year:	2009
Hybridizer:	Meilland	Color:	Medium Red
Blooms:	Single	Hardiness:	Zone 5
Fragrance:	None	Height:	3′
Comments:	AARS 2009; small, cherry red bloom with white eye		

Carefree Wonder

Class:	Shrub	Year:	1990
Hybridizer:	Meilland	Color:	Pink blend
Blooms:	Semi-double	Hardiness:	Zone 4
Fragrance:	Slight	Height:	4′- 5′
Comments:	AARS 1991; small clusters; orange hips		

Cecile Brunner

Class:	Polyantha	Year:	1881
Hybridizer:	Ducher	Color:	Light Pink
Blooms:	Double	Hardiness:	Zone 5
Fragrance:	Moderate	Height:	2′- 4′
Comments:	aka "Sweetheart Rose"; shade tolerant; small pink HT form blooms		

Celestial

Class:	Alba	Year:	Before 1810
Hybridizer:	Unknown	Color:	Light Pink
Blooms:	Semi-double	Hardiness:	Zone 5
Fragrance:	Strong	Height:	6'
Comments:	aka Celeste; likes partial shade; shell pink flowers with golden yellow stamens		

Champlain

Class:	HKor (shrub)	Year:	1982
Hybridizer:	Svejda	Color:	Dark Red
Blooms:	Double	Hardiness:	Zone 4
Fragrance:	None	Height:	4'
Comments:	Agr. Canada Explorer Series		

Charles Albanel

Class:	HRg (shrub)	Year:	1982
Hybridizer:	Svejda	Color:	Medium Red
Blooms:	Semi-double	Hardiness:	Zone 3
Fragrance:	Slight	Height:	2'
Comments:	Agr. Canada Explorer Series; ground cover		

Cherry Meidiland

Class:	Shrub	Year:	1995
Hybridizer:	Meilland	Color:	Red blend
Blooms:	Single	Hardiness:	Zone 4
Fragrance:	None	Height:	5'
Comments:	Red single with white eye		

Chuckles *

Class:	Floribunda	Year:	1958
Hybridizer:	Shepherd	Color:	Deep Pink
Blooms:	Single	Hardiness:	Zone 4
Fragrance:	Moderate	Height:	5'
Comments:	Shade tolerant		

Clair Matin *

Class:	LCl	Year:	1960
Hybridizer:	Meilland	Color:	Medium Pink
Blooms:	Semi-double	Hardiness:	Zone 5
Fragrance:	Slight	Height:	10'-15'
Comments:	Clusters of pink blooms; shade tolerant		

Climbing Pinkie *

Class:	Cl Polyantha	Year:	1952
Hybridizer:	Dering	Color:	Medium Pink
Blooms:	Semi-double	Hardiness:	Zone 6
Fragrance:	Moderate	Height:	10´
Comments:	aka Little Pinkie; Earth Kind Rose; cascading clusters of flowers		

Constance Spry

Class:	Shrub	Year:	1961
Hybridizer:	Austin	Color:	Light Pink
Blooms:	Double	Hardiness:	Zone 4
Fragrance:	Strong	Height:	6´
Comments:	First David Austin rose; myrrh fragrance; once blooming; grows 12´ as climber		

Coral Drift

Class:	Shrub	Year:	2007
Hybridizer:	Meilland	Color:	Orange-pink
Blooms:	Semi-double	Hardiness:	Zone 5
Fragrance:	None	Height:	18´´
Comments:	Continuous bloom; ground cover		

Countess Celeste

Class:	Shrub	Year:	1997
Hybridizer:	Poulsen	Color:	Orange-pink
Blooms:	Very Double	Hardiness:	Zone 5
Fragrance:	Moderate	Height:	2´-3´
Comments:	Apple fragrance		

Country Dancer

Class:	Shrub	Year:	1973
Hybridizer:	Buck	Color:	Deep Pink
Blooms:	Double	Hardiness:	Zone 5
Fragrance:	Slight	Height:	3´
Comments:	Dark green, leathery, disease-resistant foliage; shade tolerant		

Crested Moss

Class:	Centifolia	Year:	1827
Hybridizer:	Vibert	Color:	Medium Pink
Blooms:	Very Double	Hardiness:	Zone 4
Fragrance:	Strong	Height:	5´
Comments:	aka Chapeau de Napolean; Cristata; cupped blooms		

Crimson Meidiland

Class:	Shrub	Year:	2008
Hybridizer:	Meilland	Color:	Medium Red
Blooms:	Semi-double	Hardiness:	Zone 5
Fragrance:	None	Height:	2´
Comments:	Ground cover		

Cuthbert Grant

Class:	Shrub	Year:	1967
Hybridizer:	Marshall	Color:	Dark Red
Blooms:	Semi-double	Hardiness:	Zone 3/4
Fragrance:	Strong	Height:	3´
Comments:	Agr. Canada Parkland Series; deep red flowers		

Dart's Dash

Class:	HRg (shrub)	Year:	Unknown
Hybridizer:	Unknown	Color:	Dark Red
Blooms:	Semi-double	Hardiness:	Zone 3
Fragrance:	Strong	Height:	4´
Comments:	Large orange hips; good for hedges		

David Thompson

Class:	HRg (shrub)	Year:	1979
Hybridizer:	Svejda	Color:	Deep Pink
Blooms:	Double	Hardiness:	Zone 3/4
Fragrance:	Strong	Height:	5´
Comments:	Agr. Canada Explorer Series		

Dortmund *

Class:	HKor (shrub)	Year:	1955
Hybridizer:	Kordes	Color:	Medium Red
Blooms:	Single	Hardiness:	Zone 5
Fragrance:	None	Height:	12´ plus
Comments:	Grown as a climber; red with white eye, yellow stamens		

Double Knock Out

Class:	Shrub	Year:	2004
Hybridizer:	Radler	Color:	Medium Red
Blooms:	Semi-double	Hardiness:	Zone 5
Fragrance:	None	Height:	4´
Comments:	Continuous blooms; twice as many petals as Knock Out		

Earth Song

Class:	Grandiflora	Year:	1975
Hybridizer:	Buck	Color:	Deep Pink
Blooms:	Semi-double	Hardiness:	Zone 3
Fragrance:	Strong	Height:	5'
Comments:	Very cold hardy		

Easy Going

Class:	Floribunda	Year:	1999
Hybridizer:	Harkness	Color:	Yellow blend
Blooms:	Double	Hardiness:	Zone 5
Fragrance:	Moderate	Height:	4'
Comments:	Sport of Livin' Easy		

Else Poulsen

Class:	Floribunda	Year:	1924
Hybridizer:	Poulsen	Color:	Medium Pink
Blooms:	Semi-double	Hardiness:	Zone 5/6
Fragrance:	Slight	Height:	5'
Comments:	aka Joan Anderson; Earth Kind Rose		

Felicite Parmentier

Class:	Alba	Year:	1834
Hybridizer:	Parmentier	Color:	Light Pink
Blooms:	Very Double	Hardiness:	Zone 4/5
Fragrance:	Strong	Height:	4'
Comments:	Partial shade; tolerates poor soil		

Fiesta

Class:	Shrub	Year:	2007
Hybridizer:	Lim	Color:	Pink blend
Blooms:	Double-Very Double	Hardiness:	Zone 4
Fragrance:	Strong	Height:	2'- 4'
Comments:	Easy Elegance; pink and white striped flower; own-root		

Fire Meidiland

Class:	Shrub	Year:	1999
Hybridizer:	Meilland	Color:	Medium Red
Blooms:	Double	Hardiness:	Zone 5
Fragrance:	Slight	Height:	1'- 4'
Comments:	Ground cover; good for slopes and banks		

First Light *

Class:	Shrub	Year:	1998
Hybridizer:	DeVor	Color:	Light Pink
Blooms:	Single	Hardiness:	Zone 5
Fragrance:	Slight	Height:	4´
Comments:	AARS 1998; burgundy stamens		

F J Grootendorst

Class:	HRg (shrub)	Year:	1918
Hybridizer:	de Goey	Color:	Medium Red
Blooms:	Double	Hardiness:	Zone 3/4
Fragrance:	Slight	Height:	5´
Comments:	Petals have serrated edges		

Flower Carpet

Class:	Shrub	Year:	1989
Hybridizer:	Noack	Color:	Deep Pink
Blooms:	Semi-double	Hardiness:	Zone 4
Fragrance:	Slight	Height:	2´
Comments:	aka Pink Flower Carpet; ground cover		

Fragrant Lavender Simplicity

Class:	Shrub	Year:	2005
Hybridizer:	Jackson & Perkins	Color:	Mauve
Blooms:	Double	Hardiness:	Zone 5
Fragrance:	Strong	Height:	4´
Comments:	Citrus fragrance; good as a hedge		

Frau Dagmar Hartopp *

Class:	HRg (shrub)	Year:	1914
Hybridizer:	Hastrup	Color:	Light Pink
Blooms:	Single	Hardiness:	Zone 2/3
Fragrance:	Strong	Height:	4´
Comments:	aka Dagmar Hastrup; large crimson hips		

Friends Forever

Class:	Shrub	Year:	2001
Hybridizer:	Lowe	Color:	Deep Pink
Blooms:	Double	Hardiness:	Zone 4
Fragrance:	Strong	Height:	6´
Comments:	aka Forever		

Frontenac

Class:	Shrub	Year:	1992
Hybridizer:	Ogilvie	Color:	Deep Pink
Blooms:	Double	Hardiness:	Zone 3
Fragrance:	Slight	Height:	3´
Comments:	Agr. Canada Explorer Series		

Fuchsia Meidiland

Class:	Shrub	Year:	1991
Hybridizer:	Meilland	Color:	Deep Pink
Blooms:	Single	Hardiness:	Zone 4
Fragrance:	Slight	Height:	2´
Comments:	Ground cover		

George Vancouver

Class:	Shrub	Year:	1994
Hybridizer:	Ogilvie	Color:	Medium Red
Blooms:	Semi-double	Hardiness:	Zone 3
Fragrance:	Slight	Height:	3´
Comments:	Agr. Canada Explorer Series; red hips in fall		

Golden Arctic *

Class:	LCl	Year:	1954
Hybridizer:	Brownell	Color:	Med.Yellow
Blooms:	Double	Hardiness:	Zone 5
Fragrance:	Moderate	Height:	8´
Comments:	aka Everblooming Pillar No. 84; Sub-Zero rose		

Golden Unicorn

Class:	Shrub	Year:	1985
Hybridizer:	Buck	Color:	Yellow blend
Blooms:	Semi-double	Hardiness:	Zone 4
Fragrance:	Slight	Height:	4´
Comments:	Large cupped flowers		

Grandma's Blessing

Class:	Shrub	Year:	2004
Hybridizer:	Lim	Color:	Deep Pink
Blooms:	Double	Hardiness:	Zone 5
Fragrance:	Strong	Height:	2´ - 3´
Comments:	Easy Elegance; hybrid tea form blooms; own-root		

Hansa *

Class:	HRg (shrub)	Year:	1905
Hybridizer:	Schaum & Van Tol	Color:	Mauve
Blooms:	Double	Hardiness:	Zone 3
Fragrance:	Strong	Height:	4' - 5'
Comments:	Clove fragrance; red hips; shade tolerant		

Hawkeye Belle

Class:	Shrub	Year:	1975
Hybridizer:	Buck	Color:	White
Blooms:	Double	Hardiness:	Zone 4
Fragrance:	Strong	Height:	4'
Comments:	Sweet fragrant blooms		

Heart 'n' Soul *

Class:	Shrub	Year:	2001
Hybridizer:	Orard	Color:	Red blend
Blooms:	Semi-double	Hardiness:	Zone 6
Fragrance:	Slight	Height:	4'
Comments:	White flowers with red edges		

Henry Hudson

Class:	HRg (shrub)	Year:	1976
Hybridizer:	Svejda	Color:	White
Blooms:	Double	Hardiness:	Zone 2/3
Fragrance:	Strong	Height:	4'
Comments:	Agr. Canada Explorer Series; clove fragrance		

Henry Kelsey

Class:	HKor (shrub)	Year:	1984
Hybridizer:	Svejda	Color:	Medium Red
Blooms:	Semi-double	Hardiness:	Zone 3
Fragrance:	Strong	Height:	6' - 8'
Comments:	Agr. Canada Explorer Series; can be trained as climber; spicy fragrance; extremely hardy		

Heritage *

Class:	Shrub	Year:	1985
Hybridizer:	Austin	Color:	Light Pink
Blooms:	Very double	Hardiness:	Zone 5
Fragrance:	Strong	Height:	4'
Comments:	Fragrant, soft pink flowers		

Home Run *

Class:	Shrub	Year:	2006
Hybridizer:	Carruth	Color:	Medium Red
Blooms:	Single	Hardiness:	Zone 5
Fragrance:	Slight	Height:	4′
Comments:	Eye-catching, rich red blooms with golden centers		

Honey Perfume

Class:	Floribunda	Year:	2005
Hybridizer:	Zary	Color:	Apricot blend
Blooms:	Double	Hardiness:	Zone 5
Fragrance:	Strong	Height:	3′
Comments:	AARS 2004; spice fragrance		

Jens Munk

Class:	HRg (shrub)	Year:	1974
Hybridizer:	Svejda	Color:	Medium Pink
Blooms:	Semi-double	Hardiness:	Zone 2/3
Fragrance:	Strong	Height:	5′
Comments:	Agr. Canada Explorer Series; very hardy		

John Cabot *

Class:	HKor (shrub)	Year:	1978
Hybridizer:	Svejda	Color:	Medium Red
Blooms:	Semi-double	Hardiness:	Zone 3/4
Fragrance:	Slight	Height:	4′-5′
Comments:	Agr. Canada Explorer Series; as climber 6′-9′		

John Davis

Class:	HKor (shrub)	Year:	1986
Hybridizer:	Svejda	Color:	Medium Pink
Blooms:	Double	Hardiness:	Zone 3/4
Fragrance:	Strong	Height:	5′
Comments:	Agr. Canada Explorer Series		

John Franklin

Class:	Shrub	Year:	1980
Hybridizer:	Svejda	Color:	Medium Red
Blooms:	Double	Hardiness:	Zone 4
Fragrance:	Slight	Height:	3′-4′
Comments:	Agr. Canada Explorer Series; shade tolerant		

Photo Gallery of Sustainable Roses

All the Rage

Blushing Knock Out

Carefree Delight

Carefree Beauty

Ballerina

Chuckles

Clair Matin

Climbing Pinkie

Dortmund

First Light

Frau Dagmar Hartopp

Golden Arctic

Hansa

Heart 'n' Soul

Heritage

Home Run

John Cabot

Julia Child

Knock Out

Lady Elsie May

My Hero

My Girl

Macy's Pride

Nearly Wild

New Dawn

Rhode Island Red

Scarlet Meidiland

Scarlet Sensation

Royal Bonica

Sunny Knock Out

Sweet Fragrance

Therese Bugnet

White Meidiland

SUSTAINABLE ROSES FOR NEW ENGLAND • 123

White Cap

William Baffin

Yellow Submarine

Yellow Brick Road

White Out

Julia Child *

Class:	Floribunda	Year:	2004
Hybridizer:	Carruth	Color:	Med. Yellow
Blooms:	Double	Hardiness:	Zone 6
Fragrance:	Strong	Height:	4´
Comments:	AARS 2006; licorice scent; great yellow flowers		

Kiss Me

Class:	Grandiflora	Year:	2006
Hybridizer:	Lim	Color:	Medium Pink
Blooms:	Semi-double	Hardiness:	Zone 5
Fragrance:	Moderate	Height:	2´ - 3´
Comments:	Easy Elegance; clusters of fragrant blooms; own-root		

Knock Out *

Class:	Shrub	Year:	1999
Hybridizer:	Radler	Color:	Red
Blooms:	Single	Hardiness:	Zone 4/5
Fragrance:	None	Height:	5´
Comments:	AARS 2000; Earth Kind rose; very disease resistant		

Lady Elsie May *

Class:	Shrub	Year:	2002
Hybridizer:	Noack	Color:	Orange-pink
Blooms:	Semi-double	Hardiness:	Zone 5
Fragrance:	Slight	Height:	3´
Comments:	AARS 2005; floriferous		

Lambert Closse

Class:	Shrub	Year:	1994
Hybridizer:	Ogilvie	Color:	Medium Pink
Blooms:	Double	Hardiness:	Zone 3/4
Fragrance:	None	Height:	3´
Comments:	Agr. Canada Explorer Series		

Linda Campbell

Class:	HRg (shrub)	Year:	1990
Hybridizer:	Moore	Color:	Medium Red
Blooms:	Semi-double	Hardiness:	Zone 4
Fragrance:	None	Height:	6´
Comments:	Bright red blooms; nearly thornless rugosa		

Livin' Easy

Class:	Floribunda	Year:	1992
Hybridizer:	Harkness	Color:	Orange blend
Blooms:	Double	Hardiness:	Zone 5
Fragrance:	Slight	Height:	4´
Comments:	AARS 1996; ruffled orange blooms		

Macy's Pride *

Class:	Shrub	Year:	2003
Hybridizer:	Lim	Color:	White
Blooms:	Semi-double	Hardiness:	Zone 5
Fragrance:	Moderate	Height:	3´
Comments:	Easy Elegance; creamy white blooms; own-root		

Madame Hardy

Class:	Damask	Year:	1832
Hybridizer:	Hardy	Color:	White
Blooms:	Very Double	Hardiness:	Zone 4
Fragrance:	Strong	Height:	5´
Comments:	White blooms with green pip; once-blooming		

Magic Meidiland

Class:	Shrub	Year:	1993
Hybridizer:	Meilland	Color:	Medium Pink
Blooms:	Semi-double	Hardiness:	Zone 5
Fragrance:	None	Height:	2´
Comments:	Ground cover		

Marie Bugnet

Class:	HRg (shrub)	Year:	1963
Hybridizer:	Bugnet	Color:	White
Blooms:	Semi-double	Hardiness:	Zone 3
Fragrance:	Strong	Height:	4´
Comments:	Leaves not rugosa-like		

Marie Daly

Class:	Polyantha	Year:	1999
Hybridizer:	Unknown	Color:	Medium Pink
Blooms:	Semi-double	Hardiness:	Zone 5
Fragrance:	Moderate	Height:	3´
Comments:	Earth Kind rose; sport of Marie Pavie		

Marie Pavie

Class:	Polyantha	Year:	1888
Hybridizer:	Alegatiere	Color:	White
Blooms:	Semi-double	Hardiness:	Zone 5
Fragrance:	Strong	Height:	3´
Comments:	Flowers in small clusters; few thorns		

Martin Frobisher

Class:	HRg (shrub)	Year:	1968
Hybridizer:	Svejda	Color:	Light Pink
Blooms:	Semi-double	Hardiness:	Zone 3
Fragrance:	Moderate	Height:	6´
Comments:	Agr. Canada Explorer Series; shade tolerant		

Max Graf

Class:	HRg (shrub)	Year:	1919
Hybridizer:	Bowditch	Color:	Pink blend
Blooms:	Single	Hardiness:	Zone 4
Fragrance:	Strong	Height:	3´
Comments:	Once-blooming; apple scent; ground cover		

Mayor of Casterbridge

Class:	Shrub	Year:	1997
Hybridizer:	Austin	Color:	Light Pink
Blooms:	Very Double	Hardiness:	Zone 5
Fragrance:	Moderate	Height:	4´
Comments:	Very floriferous		

Mme Plantier

Class:	Alba	Year:	1835
Hybridizer:	Plantier	Color:	White
Blooms:	Very Double	Hardiness:	Zone 3/4
Fragrance:	Strong	Height:	10´
Comments:	Can be grown as climber; almost thornless		

Moje Hammarberg

Class:	HRg (shrub)	Year:	1931
Hybridizer:	Hammarberg	Color:	Mauve
Blooms:	Double	Hardiness:	Zone 3
Fragrance:	Strong	Height:	3´- 4´
Comments:	Spicy fragrance; shade tolerant		

Morden Centennial

Class:	Shrub	Year:	1980
Hybridizer:	Marshall	Color:	Medium Pink
Blooms:	Double	Hardiness:	Zone 3/4
Fragrance:	Slight	Height:	5´
Comments:	Agr. Canada Parkland Series; very hardy		

Morning Magic

Class:	LCl	Year:	2008
Hybridizer:	Radler	Color:	Light Pink
Blooms:	Single	Hardiness:	Zone 5
Fragrance:	None	Height:	6´ - 8´
Comments:	Small climber		

Mutabilis

Class:	China	Year:	before 1894
Hybridizer:	Unknown	Color:	Yellow blend
Blooms:	Single	Hardiness:	Zone 6
Fragrance:	Slight	Height:	4´ - 6´
Comments:	aka Butterfly Rose; *R. chinensis mutabilis*; flowers change from yellow to pink to dark red, looking like butterflies on the bush		

My Girl *

Class:	Shrub	Year:	2008
Hybridizer:	Lim	Color:	Deep Pink
Blooms:	Double	Hardiness:	Zone 4
Fragrance:	None	Height:	3´ - 4´
Comments:	Easy Elegance; ruffled blooms; own-root		

My Hero *

Class:	Shrub	Year:	2003
Hybridizer:	Lim	Color:	Medium Red
Blooms:	Semi-double	Hardiness:	Zone 5
Fragrance:	None	Height:	4´
Comments:	Easy Elegance; continuous blooms; own-root		

Nearly Wild *

Class:	Floribunda	Year:	1941
Hybridizer:	Brownell	Color:	Pink
Blooms:	Single	Hardiness:	Zone 4/5
Fragrance:	Slight	Height:	3´
Comments:	Continuous bloom; tolerates poor soil		

New Dawn *

Class:	LCl	Year:	1930
Hybridizer:	Dreer	Color:	Light Pink
Blooms:	Double	Hardiness:	Zone 4
Fragrance:	Moderate	Height:	10'
Comments:	aka Everblooming Dr. W. Van Fleet; World's Favorite Rose 1997; Earth Kind Rose		

Newport Fairy

Class:	HWich (rambler)	Year:	1908
Hybridizer:	Gardner	Color:	Pink blend
Blooms:	Single	Hardiness:	Zone 5
Fragrance:	None	Height:	12' - 20'
Comments:	Vigorous rambler; large clusters of pink flowers with white centers; once-blooming		

Paul Neyron

Class:	Hybrid Perpetual	Year:	1869
Hybridizer:	Levet	Color:	Medium Pink
Blooms:	Very double	Hardiness:	Zone 5
Fragrance:	Strong	Height:	4'
Comments:	Large 6''- 7'' fragrant blooms		

Peach Drift

Class:	Shrub	Year:	2006
Hybridizer:	Meilland	Color:	Apricot blend
Blooms:	Semi-double	Hardiness:	Zone 5
Fragrance:	None	Height:	1'
Comments:	Ground cover		

Perle d'Or

Class:	Polyantha	Year:	1875
Hybridizer:	Rambaux	Color:	Yellow blend
Blooms:	Very double	Hardiness:	Zone 5/6
Fragrance:	Strong	Height:	3'
Comments:	aka Yellow Cecile Brunner; Earth Kind rose		

Pink Double Knock Out

Class:	Shrub	Year:	2007
Hybridizer:	Radler	Color:	Medium Pink
Blooms:	Semi-double	Hardiness:	Zone 5
Fragrance:	Slight	Height:	4'
Comments:	More petals than Pink Knock Out		

Pink Grootendorst

Class:	HRg (shrub)	Year:	1923
Hybridizer:	Grootendorst	Color:	Medium Pink
Blooms:	Very Double	Hardiness:	Zone 3/4
Fragrance:	Slight	Height:	6´
Comments:	Small pink frilly flowers		

Pink Knock Out

Class:	Shrub	Year:	2004
Hybridizer:	Radler	Color:	Medium Pink
Blooms:	Single	Hardiness:	Zone 5
Fragrance:	Slight	Height:	4´
Comments:	Continuous blooms		

Pink Meidiland

Class:	Shrub	Year:	1985
Hybridizer:	Meilland	Color:	Pink blend
Blooms:	Single	Hardiness:	Zone 4/5
Fragrance:	Slight	Height:	4´
Comments:	Tolerates shade; single pink flower with white eye		

Pink Pavement

Class:	HRg (shrub)	Year:	1991
Hybridizer:	Baum	Color:	Orange-pink
Blooms:	Semi-double	Hardiness:	Zone 3
Fragrance:	Strong	Height:	2´
Comments:	Ground cover		

Polar Ice

Class:	HRg (shrub)	Year:	1991
Hybridizer:	Strobel	Color:	White
Blooms:	Double	Hardiness:	Zone 3/4
Fragrance:	Strong	Height:	4´
Comments:	aka Polareis; once-blooming		

Polar Joy

Class:	Shrub	Year:	2005
Hybridizer:	Lim	Color:	Light Pink
Blooms:	Single	Hardiness:	Zone 4
Fragrance:	None	Height:	5´ - 6´
Comments:	aka Northern Encore; own-root tree rose (available as 3´ & 6´ standards)		

Prairie Dawn

Class:	Shrub	Year:	1959
Hybridizer:	Morden	Color:	Medium Pink
Blooms:	Semi-double	Hardiness:	Zone 3
Fragrance:	None	Height:	8'
Comments:	Agr. Canada Parkland Series; very hardy		

Prairie Joy

Class:	Shrub	Year:	1990
Hybridizer:	Collicutt	Color:	Medium Pink
Blooms:	Double	Hardiness:	Zone 3
Fragrance:	Slight	Height:	4'
Comments:	Agr. Canada Parkland Series; very hardy		

Prairie Princess

Class:	Shrub	Year:	1972
Hybridizer:	Buck	Color:	Orange-pink
Blooms:	Semi-double	Hardiness:	Zone 4/5
Fragrance:	Moderate	Height:	5' - 6'
Comments:	Can be trained as a climber		

Prairie Sunrise

Class:	Shrub	Year:	1997
Hybridizer:	Buck	Color:	Apricot blend
Blooms:	Very Double	Hardiness:	Zone 4/5
Fragrance:	Strong	Height:	3'
Comments:	Old-fashioned form; 50+ petals		

Pretty Lady

Class:	Floribunda	Year:	1996
Hybridizer:	Scrivens	Color:	Light Pink
Blooms:	Semi-double	Hardiness:	Zone 5
Fragrance:	Moderate	Height:	4'
Comments:	Rounded, neat habit; lovely blooms		

Purple Pavement

Class:	HRg (shrub)	Year:	1984
Hybridizer:	Baum	Color:	Mauve
Blooms:	Single	Hardiness:	Zone 3/4
Fragrance:	Strong	Height:	3'
Comments:	aka Rotesmeer; dark red hips		

Queen Elizabeth

Class:	Grandiflora	Year:	1954
Hybridizer:	Lammerts	Color:	Medium Pink
Blooms:	Double	Hardiness:	Zone 5
Fragrance:	Moderate	Height:	6'
Comments:	World's Favorite Rose 1979; AARS 1955		

Rainbow Knock Out

Class:	Shrub	Year:	2007
Hybridizer:	Radler	Color:	Pink blend
Blooms:	Single	Hardiness:	Zone 5
Fragrance:	None	Height:	3'
Comments:	AARS 2007; pink with bright yellow centers		

Red Meidiland

Class:	Shrub	Year:	1989
Hybridizer:	Meilland	Color:	Red blend
Blooms:	Single	Hardiness:	Zone 4
Fragrance:	None	Height:	2'
Comments:	Ground cover; red flower with white eye		

Rhode Island Red *

Class:	LCl	Year:	1957
Hybridizer:	Brownell	Color:	Dark Red
Blooms:	Double	Hardiness:	Zone 5
Fragrance:	Moderate	Height:	10'
Comments:	Deep red flowers; also can be grown as bush; Sub-Zero rose		

Rosa gallica versicolor

Class:	Species	Year:	Before 1581
Hybridizer:	None	Color:	Pink blend
Blooms:	Single	Hardiness:	Zone 4/5
Fragrance:	Strong	Height:	3'
Comments:	aka Rosa Mundi; once-blooming striped rose		

Rosa roxburghii

Class:	Species	Year:	Before 1814
Hybridizer:	None	Color:	Medium Pink
Blooms:	Semi-double	Hardiness:	Zone 5/6
Fragrance:	Moderate	Height:	6'
Comments:	aka Chestnut Rose, Burr Rose; sporadic repeat; very thorny		

Rosa rubrifolia

Class:	Species	Year:	1789
Hybridizer:	None	Color:	Medium Pink
Blooms:	Single	Hardiness:	Zone 2/3
Fragrance:	None	Height:	6'
Comments:	aka *R. glauca*, Red Leaf Rose; once-blooming		

Rosa rugosa alba

Class:	Species	Year:	1784
Hybridizer:	None	Color:	White
Blooms:	Single	Hardiness:	Zone 2/3
Fragrance:	Moderate	Height:	4'- 6'
Comments:	Large reddish orange hips		

Rosa rugosa rubra

Class:	Species	Year:	1784
Hybridizer:	None	Color:	Mauve
Blooms:	Single	Hardiness:	Zone 2/3
Fragrance:	Moderate	Height:	4'
Comments:	Shade tolerant; large orange-red hips		

Rose de Rescht

Class:	Portland	Year:	1880
Hybridizer:	Unknown	Color:	Deep Pink
Blooms:	Very Double	Hardiness:	Zone 4/5
Fragrance:	Very Strong	Height:	3'
Comments:	Extremely fragrant rosette-shaped blooms		

Royal Bonica *

Class:	Shrub	Year:	1994
Hybridizer:	Meilland	Color:	Medium Pink
Blooms:	Very Double	Hardiness:	Zone 5
Fragrance:	Slight	Height:	3'- 4'
Comments:	Sport of Bonica		

Ruby Meidiland

Class:	Shrub	Year:	2002
Hybridizer:	Meilland	Color:	Medium Red
Blooms:	Semi-double	Hardiness:	Zone 4
Fragrance:	Slight	Height:	2'- 3'
Comments:	Continuous blooms; clusters		

Salet

Class:	Moss	Year:	1854
Hybridizer:	Lacharme	Color:	Medium Pink
Blooms:	Very Double	Hardiness:	Zone 5
Fragrance:	Strong	Height:	4'
Comments:	Repeat flowering moss rose		

Sally Holmes

Class:	HMsk (shrub)	Year:	1976
Hybridizer:	Baden-Baden	Color:	White
Blooms:	Single	Hardiness:	Zone 4/5
Fragrance:	Moderate	Height:	5'
Comments:	Grown as climber; ivory buds		

Scarlet Meidiland *

Class:	Shrub	Year:	1987
Hybridizer:	Meilland	Color:	Medium Red
Blooms:	Semi-double	Hardiness:	Zone 4/5
Fragrance:	None	Height:	3'
Comments:	Ground cover; shade tolerant; red hips		

Scarlet Sensation *

Class:	LCl	Year:	1954
Hybridizer:	Brownell	Color:	Dark Pink
Blooms:	Double	Hardiness:	Zone 5
Fragrance:	Moderate	Height:	8'
Comments:	aka Everblooming Pillar No. 73; Sub-Zero rose		

Sea Foam

Class:	Shrub	Year:	1964
Hybridizer:	Schwartz	Color:	White
Blooms:	Very Double	Hardiness:	Zone 4/5
Fragrance:	Slight	Height:	4'
Comments:	Earth Kind Rose; vigorous with masses of blooms		

Sevilliana

Class:	Shrub	Year:	1976
Hybridizer:	Buck	Color:	Pink blend
Blooms:	Semi-double	Hardiness:	Zone 4
Fragrance:	Moderate	Height:	4'
Comments:	Constant blooms; bright red hips		

Shropshire Lass

Class:	Shrub	Year:	1968
Hybridizer:	Austin	Color:	Light Pink
Blooms:	Single	Hardiness:	Zone 4/5
Fragrance:	Moderate	Height:	8´
Comments:	Once-blooming, large single blooms		

Sunny Knock Out *

Class:	Shrub	Year:	2007
Hybridizer:	Radler	Color:	Light Yellow
Blooms:	Single	Hardiness:	Zone 5
Fragrance:	Slight	Height:	3´
Comments:	Very disease resistant		

Super Hero

Class:	Floribunda	Year:	2008
Hybridizer:	Lim	Color:	Medium Red
Blooms:	Double	Hardiness:	Zone 4
Fragrance:	None	Height:	4´
Comments:	Easy Elegance; very disease resistant; own-root		

Sweet Fragrance *

Class:	Grandiflora	Year:	2007
Hybridizer:	Lim	Color:	Apricot blend
Blooms:	Double	Hardiness:	Zone 5
Fragrance:	Slight	Height:	4´
Comments:	Easy Elegance; great color; own-root		

Teasing Georgia

Class:	Shrub	Year:	1998
Hybridizer:	Austin	Color:	Med. Yellow
Blooms:	Very Double	Hardiness:	Zone 5
Fragrance:	Strong	Height:	4´
Comments:	Tea rose fragrance		

The Fairy

Class:	Polyantha	Year:	1932
Hybridizer:	Bentall	Color:	Light Pink
Blooms:	Semi-double	Hardiness:	Zone 4
Fragrance:	None	Height:	3´
Comments:	Earth Kind Rose; small, pompom-shaped flowers grow in clusters		

The Mayflower

Class:	Shrub	Year:	2002
Hybridizer:	Austin	Color:	Medium Pink
Blooms:	Very Double	Hardiness:	Zone 4
Fragrance:	Strong	Height:	4´
Comments:	2-inch pink blooms; very fragrant		

Therese Bugnet *

Class:	HRg (shrub)	Year:	1950
Hybridizer:	Bugnet	Color:	Medium Pink
Blooms:	Double	Hardiness:	Zone 3
Fragrance:	Strong	Height:	6´
Comments:	Very hardy; dark red canes in winter		

Wasagaming

Class:	HRg (shrub)	Year:	1939
Hybridizer:	Skinner	Color:	Medium Pink
Blooms:	Very Double	Hardiness:	Zone 3
Fragrance:	Strong	Height:	3´
Comments:	Very hardy; fragrant blooms		

Westerland

Class:	Shrub	Year:	1970
Hybridizer:	Kordes	Color:	Apricot blend
Blooms:	Semi-double	Hardiness:	Zone 5
Fragrance:	Moderate	Height:	10´- 12´
Comments:	A shrub that grows like a climber		

White Cap *

Class:	LCl	Year:	1954
Hybridizer:	Brownell	Color:	White
Blooms:	Very Double	Hardiness:	Zone 5
Fragrance:	Slight	Height:	8´
Comments:	aka Everblooming Pillar No. 3; Sub-Zero rose		

White Flower Carpet

Class:	Floribunda	Year:	1991
Hybridizer:	Noack	Color:	White
Blooms:	Semi-double	Hardiness:	Zone 6
Fragrance:	Strong	Height:	2´
Comments:	aka Flower Carpet Blanc; ground cover		

White Grootendorst

Class:	HRg (shrub)	Year:	1962
Hybridizer:	Eddy	Color:	White
Blooms:	Double	Hardiness:	Zone 3/4
Fragrance:	Slight	Height:	4´
Comments:	Sport of Pink Grootendorst; tolerates some shade		

White Meidiland *

Class:	Shrub	Year:	1987
Hybridizer:	Meilland	Color:	White
Blooms:	Double	Hardiness:	Zone 4
Fragrance:	None	Height:	2´
Comments:	Ground cover; tolerates shade		

White Out *

Class:	Shrub	Year:	2009
Hybridizer:	Radler	Color:	White
Blooms:	Single	Hardiness:	Zone 5
Fragrance:	None	Height:	3´
Comments:	Striking white flowers bloom all season		

William Baffin *

Class:	HKor (shrub)	Year:	1983
Hybridizer:	Svejda	Color:	Deep Pink
Blooms:	Semi-double	Hardiness:	Zone 2/3
Fragrance:	Slight	Height:	8´
Comments:	Agr. Canada Explorer Series; can be grown as climber		

William Shakespeare 2000

Class:	Shrub	Year:	2001
Hybridizer:	Austin	Color:	Dark Red
Blooms:	Very Double	Hardiness:	Zone 5
Fragrance:	Strong	Height:	3´
Comments:	Velvety deep red blooms; strong rose fragrance		

Winter Sunset

Class:	Shrub	Year:	1995
Hybridizer:	Buck	Color:	Yellow blend
Blooms:	Double	Hardiness:	Zone 4/5
Fragrance:	Strong	Height:	4´
Comments:	Strong fruity fragrance		

Yellow Brick Road *

Class:	Shrub	Year:	2007
Hybridizer:	Lim	Color:	Deep Yellow
Blooms:	Double	Hardiness:	Zone 5
Fragrance:	None	Height:	2' - 3'
Comments:	Easy Elegance; clusters of old-fashioned blooms, own-root		

Yellow Submarine *

Class:	Shrub	Year:	2004
Hybridizer:	Lim	Color:	Med. Yellow
Blooms:	Double	Hardiness:	Zone 5
Fragrance:	None	Height:	4'
Comments:	Easy Elegance; soft yellow, long lasting flowers; own-root		

Zephirine Drouhin

Class:	Bourbon	Year:	1868
Hybridizer:	Bizot	Color:	Medium Pink
Blooms:	Double	Hardiness:	Zone 5/6
Fragrance:	Moderate	Height:	10' - 12'
Comments:	Usually grown as a climber; thornless; shade tolerant		

Abbreviation Key

AARS	All America Rose Selection
A	Alba
Agr. Canada	Agriculture Canada
aka	Also Known As
B	Bourbon
C	Centifolia
Ch	China
Cl HT	Climbing Hybrid Tea
Cl Pol	Climbing Polyantha
Cl	Climber
D	Damask
F	Floribunda
G	Gallica
Gr	Grandiflora
HKor (S)	Hybrid Kordesii
HMsk (S)	Hybrid Musk
HP	Hybrid Perpetual
HRg (S)	Hybrid Rugosa
HT	Hybrid Tea
HWich (R)	Hybrid Wichurana
LCl	Large-Flowered Climber
M	Moss
Min	Miniature
P	Portland
Pol	Polyantha
R	Rambler
S	Shrub
Sp	Species

Appendix 1

Anatomy of a Rose

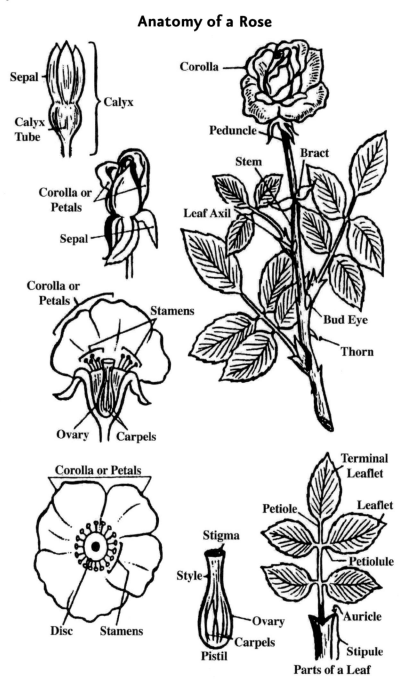

Courtesy of American Rose Society

Appendix 2

Rose Societies in New England & Eastern Canada

Rose Societies are great sources of information and a way to learn about how to grow roses in your geographical area. Most rose societies have monthly meetings, sponsor a yearly rose show and have a newsletter to keep their membership informed. Another advantage to belonging to a local rose society is members may be entitled to discounts at rose nurseries and garden centers.

The following are all members of the Yankee District (www.arsyankee.org) of the American Rose Society (www.ars.org).

Connecticut Rose Society	www.ctrose.org
Lower Cape Rose Society	www.lowercaperosesociety.org
Maine Rose Society	www.mainerosesociety.com
Mid-Maine Rose Society	No website
New England Rose Society	www.rosepetals.org
New Hampshire Rose Society	www.newhampshirerosesociety.org
Rhode Island Rose Society	www.rirs.org
Societe du Roses du Quebec	www.rosesquebec.org

Appendix 3

Public Rose Gardens in New England & Eastern Canada

We include a list of public rose gardens in New England and eastern Canada. Some of these gardens are All-American Rose Selection Test Gardens (AARS). Many of these gardens are free and others charge an entry fee.

Connecticut

Boothe Wedding Rose Garden, Boothe Memorial Park & Museum, Stratford, CT
Elizabeth Park Rose Garden (AARS Test Garden), West Hartford, CT
Norwich Memorial Rose Garden, Norwich, CT
Pardee Rose Garden, East Rock Park, Hamden, CT

Maine

Rose Circle, Deering Oaks Park, Portland, ME
Merryspring Rose Garden, Merryspring Nature Center, Camden, ME

Massachusetts

James P. Kelleher Rose Garden, Boston, MA
Millie & Tip O'Neill Rose Garden, Harwich Community Center, Harwich, MA
Stanley Park (AARS Test Garden), Westfield, MA

New Hampshire

Fuller Gardens Rose Gardens, North Hampton, NH

Rhode Island

Roger Williams Park Victorian Rose Garden, Providence, RI
Chet Clayton Sustainable Rose Garden, University of Rhode Island Botanical Gardens, Kingston, RI

Canada

Rose Garden, Montreal Botanical Garden, Montreal, Canada

Bibliography

Beales, Peter, *Classic Roses*. Henry Holt & Co., Inc., 1997

Cairns, Dr. Tommy. *Ortho's All About Roses*. Meredith Books, 1999

Capon, Brian. *Botany for Gardeners*. Timber Press, 1990

Chute, Angelina P., Editor, *Rhode Island Rose Society Rose Grower's Guide*. Rhode Island Rose Society, Inc., 2004

Chute, Angelina. "Winterizing Woes." *Rhode Island Rose Review*. Rhode Island Rose Society, Inc., November 2004

Chute, Michael. "Basic Rose Gardening: Six Easy to Follow Steps to Successful Rose Gardening." *Rhode Island Rose Review,* Rhode Island Rose Society, Inc., April 2001

Chute, Mike. "Seafood for Roses." *Rhode Island Rose Review*. Rhode Island Rose Society, Inc., May 2003

Consulting Rosarian Manual, 2nd Edition. The American Rose Society, July 2001

Druitt, Liz. *The Organic Rose Garden*. Taylor Publishing Co., 1996

Ellis, Barbara W. *The Organic Gardener's Handbook of Natural Insect and Disease Control*. Rodale Press, Inc., 1996

Macoboy, Stirling. *The Ultimate Rose Book*. Harry N. Abrams, Inc., 1993

Marinelli, Janet, Editor, *Brooklyn Botanic Garden Natural Disease Control*. BBG, Inc., 2000

McKinley, Michael, ed. *Ortho's Complete Guide to Roses*. Meredith Books, 2004

Olds, Margaret, *Botanica's Rose: The Encyclopedia of Roses*. Mynah, Random House, Australia, 1998

Osborne, Robert. *Hardy Roses*. Garden Way Publishing, Storey Communications, Inc., 1991

Parker, Sybil P., Editor. *Rhode Island Sustainable Gardening Manual*. University of Rhode Island, 2006

Ray, Richard, Michael MacCaskey. *Roses How to Select, Grow and Enjoy*. Fisher Publishing, Inc., 1981

Scanniello, Stephen. *Jackson & Perkins Rose Companion: Growing Annuals, Perennials, Bulbs, Shrubs, and Vines with Roses*. Cool Springs Press, 2004

Smiley, Beth, Ray Rogers, Editors. *Ultimate Rose,* American Rose Society. Dorling Kindersley Publishing, Inc., 2000

Stell, Elizabeth P. *Secrets to Great Soil*. Storey Communications, Inc., 1998

Thomas, Graham. *Garden of Roses*. Salem House, 1987

Walheim, Lance and the Editors at the National Gardening Association. *Roses for Dummies, 2nd Edition*. IDG Books Worldwide, Inc., 2000

Wilde, Barbara. *Growing Roses Organically*. Rodale Press, Inc., 2002

Index

A

AARS 26, 103, 105, 107, 112, 115, 124-125, 131, 138, 141
abbreviation key
 classification 31
 sustainable rose list 138
alba roses 19
All America Rose Selection. See AARS
American Rose Society 11, 13, 14, 16, 24, 26, 28, 140
Anatomy of a Rose 139
anthracnose 73
aphids 45, 52, 63, 65-68
Asiatic beetles 66
attar of roses 14, 19
Austin, David 13

B

backfill 82-83
bacterial infections 71
Bailey Nurseries 26, 100
bareroot roses 38, 81, 84
 planting 81
beneficial microorganisms 43
blackspot 21-22, 37, 51-52, 70-73
blind shoots 66, 68
bloom cycle 9, 48, 58, 88, 92
 timing 88
Boerner, Eugene 24
bone meal 81-82
botrytis 71, 73
Bourbon roses 21
Brownell, Walter & Josephine 28, 100
Buck, Griffith 26, 100
Buck roses 26

bud eyes 39, 90
bud union 29, 39, 90, 96-97
burnt foliage 64

C

cabbage roses. See centifolia roses
Canadian Explorer roses 26, 40, 100, 102, 106, 108, 110, 113-115, 124, 126, 136
Canadian Parkland roses 110, 127, 130
cane borers 66-68, 92
canker 71, 74, 90
Carruth, Tom 10
centifolia roses 19
China roses 17, 20
chlorosis 60
classic shrubs 26
classification 16-31
climbing roses 28, 79, 94
 winter protection 97
color 10-11
color classes 11
companion planting 63
compost 80, 96
compound leaves 92
container-grown roses 39, 52
 planting 84
container roses 52
 winter protection 97
cribs 97
crown gall 71, 74

D

damask roses 18
dead, diseased, damaged canes 87-88, 90-91
deadheading 10, 91-92, 95

defoliation 72
desiccate 96-97
disbudding 93
disease resistance 25-27, 36-38, 62, 65, 100-101
disease resistant. See disease resistance
diseases 62, 70-75, 96
 causes & solutions 72
dormancy 47, 58, 85, 88, 94-96, 98
dormant. See dormancy
double roses 102
downy mildew 74
drip irrigation 52
drip line 59

E

EarthKind™ 101
Easy Elegance roses 26-27, 100, 103, 111, 113, 124-125, 127, 134, 137
everblooming 9, 29, 86-87, 92, 101
everblooming pillars 28
Explorer roses. See Canadian Explorer roses

F

fertilizer 62
fertilizers, type 56
 inorganic 56
 organic 56
 slow release 56
 water soluble 56
fertilizing 55-60
fertilizing program 57
finger prune 93
floribundas 9, 24, 79, 95, 101
foliage 13

foliar feed 56
fragrance 13-15
fungal diseases 36, 47, 70-71, 79, 99-100
fungicides 64, 71

G

gallica roses 18
Gamble Fragrance Award 14-15
garden journal 64
grades of roses 39
grafted rose 39
grafting 39
grandifloras 25, 79, 95
growth bud 90, 92
growth habit 37, 79, 101

H

hardiness zones. *See* zones
heeling in 81
hilling up 96
honeydew 67
horse manure 43, 96
hybrid perpetual roses 22
hybrid rugosa roses 27
hybrid tea form 12, 24
hybrid tea roses 9, 23, 79, 95, 100
hybrid wichuranas 28-29

I

insects 65-70
  beneficial 65, 69
  destructive 63, 65-66
  symptoms & controls 67
insects & diseases 61-75
  chemical option 64
  combined approach 65
  organic option 62
  plant sustainable varieties 61
insecticidal soap 63
insecticides 63-64
integrated pest management 61

J

Jackson & Perkins 24
Japanese beetles 5, 66, 69

L

large-flowered climbers 9, 29, 101
lateral shoots 91
leaf axil 92
leaflet 92
leafrollers 66, 70
Lim, Ping 26, 29, 100
lime 42, 46, 80, 96
  calcitic 42
  dolomitic 42
loam. *See* topsoil

M

macronutrients 45, 55
mannitol 45
manure. *See* horse manure
Meilland International 26, 100
microclimates 48, 95, 101
micronutrients 45, 55-56
microorganisms 58, 88
midge 66, 68
midges. *See* midge
miniature roses 9, 27, 79
  planting 84
Mini-Flora roses 28
miticides 64, 69
modern roses 23-30
modern shrubs 26
Montreal Botanical Garden 22
Moore, Ralph 27
moss roses 19
mudding in 83
mulch 44-45, 51, 72, 96
  inorganic 44
  organic 44

N

new wood 87
New England USDA Plant Hardiness Zones 35
nitrogen 55
Noisette roses 22
NPK ration 56
nutrients 55, 88

O

OGRs. *See* old garden roses
old garden roses 9, 17-22, 31, 79, 94-95, 99, 101
old wood 87-88, 91
once-blooming 9, 18-19, 29, 86-88, 91-92, 101
organic amendments 43, 80
organics 46, 51, 62, 96, 97
overhead sprinklers 52
own-root roses 29, 40

P

pesticides 26-27, 36, 54, 64, 66, 79, 99-101
petal count 12, 102
  double roses 12
  semi-double roses 12
  single roses 12, 17, 25
  very double roses 12, 25
pH 42-43, 60, 62, 96
  testing pH 43
phosphorous 55
photosynthesis 47
pith 66-67, 90-91
planting 78-85, 94
  bareroot roses 81
  container-grown roses 84
  miniature roses 84
polyanthas 24, 101
polymers 53
Portland roses 21
potassium 55
potassium bicarbonate-based fungicides 63

Poulsen 24
powdery mildew 71, 73
provence roses. *See* centifolia roses
pruning 86-93, 96
　climbing roses 91
　everblooming roses 88
　floribundas 91
　how to 90
　hybrid teas & grandifloras 91
　miniature roses 91
　once-blooming roses 91
　shrub, old garden, & species roses 91
　spring pruning 86
pruning tools 89
public rose gardens 141

R
Radler, William 26
rain barrel 53
rainwater 53
raised beds 46, 80
ramblers 9, 73. *See* hybrid wichuranas
recurrent. *See* repeat blooming
repeat blooming 9, 18, 20-21, 23-25
root ball 84-85
root burn 59
rooting 39
rootstock 39
root zone 50-51, 60
rose canker 71, 74
rose catalogs 38
rose collars 96
rose cones 96
rose hips 17, 93
rose mosaic virus 75
rose societies 140
rugosa roses 13, 17, 27, 64, 95
rust 75

S
seaweed 45, 96
selecting roses 34-40
semi-double roses 102
shapes 12
shrub roses 9, 25, 79, 94-95, 99, 101
single roses 102
size 37, 79
snow 96
soaker hoses 52
softwood cuttings 40
soil 41-46, 51, 56, 58, 62, 80, 95, 97-98
soil conditioner 45
soil drench 56
soil test 56
species roses 9, 16-17, 31, 94, 101
spider mites 52, 63, 66-67, 69
spittlebugs 66, 68
sports 19, 28-29
spring pruning 86, 88
standards. *See* tree roses
Sub-Zero roses 100, 113, 131, 133, 135
suckers 90
sunlight 47-49, 62, 78
superphosphate 81-82
sustainability 5, 36, 37, 100-101
sustainable garden 26, 79
sustainable roses 99-137
Sustainable Roses for New England 102
　Photo Gallery 116
Svejda, Dr. Felicitas 100

T
tea roses 17, 20
terminal bud 93
thermal blankets 96-97
thrips 67-69

topsoil 41
transpiration 50
transplanting roses 85
tree roses 29

U
understock. *See* rootstock
USDA Plant Hardiness Zone Map 34

V
very double roses 102

W
water 50-54; 56, 62-63
　how to water 51
water crystals. *See* polymers
Weeks Roses 10
winter hardiness 26, 34, 36, 94-95, 99-100
winterkill 94-97
winter protection 90, 94-98
　methods 96

Z
zones 34-35, 94, 97, 100

Book Order Form

Please send me _____ copies of
Roses for New England—A Guide to Sustainable Rose Gardening
for $18.95 per copy (U.S.) plus $4.95 per copy for shipping.
RI residents add 7% Sales Tax to the total.

Name _____

Street Address _____

City, State, Zip _____

E-mail Address _____

Telephone _____

☐ Please autograph this book.

☐ Please sign this as a gift to

_____

Send check or money order made payable to RoseSolutions and mail to:

Rosesolutions
64 Forbes St.
Riverside, RI 02915

Books may also be ordered from www.rosesolutions.net